Descriptive Cataloging of Ancient, Medieval, Renaissance, and Early Modern Manuscripts

Gregory A. Pass

Bibliographic Standards Committee
Rare Books and Manuscripts Section

Association of College and Research Libraries
A Division of the American Library Association
Chicago 2003

The paper used in this publication meets the minimum requirements of American National Standard for Information Sciences–Permanence of Paper for Printed Library Materials, ANSI Z39.48-1992. ∞

Library of Congress Cataloging-in-Publication Data
Pass, Gregory A.
   Descriptive cataloging of ancient, medieval, Renaissance, and early modern manuscripts / Gregory A. Pass.
       p. cm.
"Bibliographic Standards Committee, Rare Books and Manuscripts Section, Association of College and Research Libraries, American Library Association."
Includes bibliographical references and index.
   ISBN 0-8389-8218-2 (alk. paper)
  1. Cataloging of manuscripts. I. Association of College and Research Libraries. Rare Books and Manuscripts Section. Bibliographic Standards Committee. II. Title.

Z695.5 .P37 2003
025.3'412--dc21

2002152837

Printed on recycled paper.

Printed in the United States of America.

07 06 05 04 03   5 4 3 2 1

Contents

ACKNOWLEDGEMENTS

The formulation of cataloging guidelines is not a task that can be accomplished unilaterally. Cataloging conventions need to reflect consensus, and in an area where the nature of the material is so diverse and the variety of approaches to its cataloging so wide consensus can be difficult to achieve. A great debt is owed, therefore, to the many people from the library and academic communities who have so generously contributed their expertise and critical judgment to the development of these guidelines.

These guidelines originated and were developed as part of a project entitled *Electronic Access to Medieval Manuscripts* (*EAMMS*), funded by the Andrew W. Mellon Foundation. The goal of the *Electronic Access* project—allied with another Mellon-sponsored project, *Digital Scriptorium*—was to devise electronic cataloging methods that would increase the ability of researchers "to access medieval manuscript catalog records, research information, images, text and tools" in a manner more effective than traditional print based resources.[1] In order to achieve this end, an international body of manuscript specialists made up of catalogers, historians, art historians, and curators from the library and academic communities was brought together to participate and advise in the project. The immediate tasks were to establish a common set of elements that would constitute a standard set of descriptive details making up the catalog record, and then to articulate how this information should be encoded. Two encoding strategies were pursued: Machine Readable Cataloging (MARC) and Standard Generalized Markup Language (SGML). The MARC initiative, which was based at the Vatican Film Library, Saint Louis University, sought to adapt the existing MARC record structure and to develop cataloging guidelines appropriate for manuscript codices that would be compatible with Anglo-American cataloging practices.[2] These guidelines received further criticism and development within the Bibliographic Stan-

---

1. *Electronic Access to Medieval Manuscripts: A Proposal to the Andrew W. Mellon Foundation from the Hill Monastic Manuscript Library, April 24, 1996*, 1. Much of the earlier work in on-line cataloging of medieval manuscripts immediately leading up to the *Electronic Access* project can be found in Menso Folkerts and Andreas Kühne, eds., *The Use of Computers in Cataloging Medieval and Renaissance Manuscripts: Papers from the International Workshop in Munich, 10–12 August 1989*, Algorismus, 4 (Munich: Institut für Geschichte der Naturwissenschaften, 1990); Hope Mayo, ed., *MARC Cataloguing for Medieval Manuscripts*, a special issue of *Rare Books & Manuscripts Librarianship* 6, no. 1 (1990); and Wesley M. Stevens, ed., *Bibliographic Access to Medieval and Renaissance Manuscripts: A Survey of Computerized Data Bases and Information Services* (New York: Haworth Press, 1992).

2. For earlier exploration of MARC applications in cataloging medieval manuscripts, see in particular the work of Hope Mayo: "Standards for Description, Indexing and Retrieval in Computerized Catalogs of Medieval Manuscripts," in Folkerts and Kühne, eds., *Use of Computers in Cataloging Medieval and Renaissance Manuscripts*, 19–39; "Introduction: MARC Cataloguing for Medieval Manuscripts," and "Medieval Manuscript Cataloging and the MARC Format," in Mayo, ed., *MARC Cataloguing for Medieval Manuscripts*, 7–9, 11–22; and "MARC Cataloguing for Medieval Manuscripts: An Evaluation," in Stevens, ed., *Bibliographic Access to Medieval and Renaissance Manuscripts*, 93–152. MARC has also been used for cataloging Greek papyri and other manuscript formats; see Peter van Minnen, "Introducing the Online Catalogue of the Duke Papyrus Collection," *Bulletin of the American Society of Papyrologists* 31 (1994): 159–170; and Elizabeth Yakel, "Pushing MARC-AMC to its Limits: The Vatican Archives Project," *American Archivist* 55 (1992): 192–201. Earlier systematic formulations of *AACR2R*-conformant cataloging guidelines and MARC encoding procedures were devised by Laurence S. Creider and David J. White, *Proposed University of Pennsylvania Codex Manuscript Cataloging Guidelines* (draft 8/31/95), and Biblioteca Apostolica Vaticana, *Formato USMARC per manoscritti e materiale d'archivio* (bozza, dicembre 1996).

dards Committee of the Rare Books and Manuscripts Section of the Association of College and Research Libraries, a division of the American Library Association; in additional to which they were reviewed by a special task force of the Committee on Cataloging: Description and Access of the Association for Library Collections & Technical Services, a division of the American Library Association. They were then finally approved by the Executive Committee of the Rare Books and Manuscripts Section of the Association of College and Research Libraries.

Among individuals involved in the development of these guidelines, none deserves greater credit for his advocacy of the application of MARC to medieval manuscript cataloging than Laurence S. Creider. Himself the author of an earlier cataloging code for medieval manuscripts at the University of Pennsylvania and the prime mover behind the collaboration of the EAMMS MARC initiative and the ACRL/RBMS Bibliographic Standards Committee, he has been closely involved in every stage of the formulation of the present guidelines, reading and commenting upon successive drafts to their great profit. He combines the special skills of a medievalist and librarian and his guidance has been invaluable. Elizabeth O'Keefe and Maria Oldal, who possess a fine knowledge of the requirements of medieval manuscripts in an automated cataloging environment and but for whose unflagging support and criticism this document would be much poorer, are also to be thanked. The earlier contributions of Hope Mayo to MARC cataloging of medieval manuscripts are also to be recognized. The directors of the EAMMS project, Consuelo Dutschke and Eric Hollas, have earned the thanks of all involved for bringing together and coordinating the efforts of an international group of manuscript specialists.

Members of the Electronic Access to Medieval Manuscripts project were Frances Benham, Melissa Conway, Laurence S. Creider, Consuelo Dutschke, Belinda Egan, Eric Hollas, Jack Marler, Hope Mayo, Gregory Pass, Ambrogio Piazzoni, Dominique Poirel, Merrilee Proffitt, Lilian Randall, Richard Rouse, Rachel Stockdale, and Theresa Vann.

Members of the Bibliographic Standards Committee during the development of these guidelines were Ann Copeland, Laurence S. Creider, Sarah Schmidt Fisher, Jain Fletcher, Jane Gillis, James Larrabee, Deborah J. Leslie, Robert Maxwell, Juliet McLaren, Richard Noble, Gregory Pass, Elizabeth Robinson, Jennifer O'Brien Roper, Beth Russell, Patrick Russell, Sandra Sider, Stephen Skuce, Eileen Smith, Joe A. Springer, Bruce Tabb, and Manon Théroux.

Members of the task force of the Committee on Cataloging: Description and Access were Thomas L. Amos, Matthew Beacom, Melissa Conway, Brad Eden, Daniel W. Kinney, Gertrude Koh, Gabriele I. Kupitz, and Maria Oldal.

Other individuals deserving special mention for providing lively and profitable discussion and valuable comment on a range of topics are Bernadette Archer, Michelle Brown, Peter Kidd, Svato Schutzner, Heather Wolfe, and Laetitia Yeandle; as well as colleagues at the Vatican Film Library and Saint Louis University including Richard Amelung, Charles Croissant, Susan L'Engle, Charles Ermatinger, Jack Marler, Michael Sinner, and Anna Zaidman.

Support from the Andrew W. Mellon Foundation, Saint Louis University, and Pius XII Memorial Library has been essential to the success of this project. The Mellon Foundation generously provided funding for three years, from 1996 to 1999. Alice B. Hayes, Executive Vice President and Provost for Saint Louis University, vigorously supported the university library and created an atmosphere in which a project such as this could flourish. And finally, it was Frances Benham, University Librarian, who was responsible for initiating the development of MARC cataloging for medieval manuscripts at Saint Louis University through a conference held at the Vatican Film Library in 1994 that has culminated in the present guidelines. Her ongoing support and interest are greatly appreciated.

Gregory A. Pass
Vatican Film Library
Saint Louis University

ABBREVIATIONS

AACR2R

Anglo-American Cataloguing Rules, 2nd ed., rev. (Ottawa: Canadian Library Association; Chicago: American Library Association, 1988).

Alexander and De la Mare,
Italian Mss.

J.J.G. Alexander and A.C. de la Mare, *The Italian Manuscripts in the Library of Major J.R. Abbey* (New York: Praeger, 1969).

AMREMM

Gregory A. Pass, *Descriptive Cataloging of Ancient, Medieval, Renaissance, and Early Modern Manuscripts* (Chicago: Association of College and Research Libraries, 2003).

APPM

Steven L. Hensen, *Archives, Personal Papers, and Manuscripts: A Cataloging Manual for Archival Repositories, Historical Societies, and Manuscript Libraries*, 2nd ed. (Chicago: Society of American Archivists, 1989).

BnF, *Manuscrits, 1983–1992*

Bibliothèque nationale de France, *Manuscrits du Moyen Âge et de la Renaissance: Enrichissements du département des manuscrits, fonds européens, 1983–92* (Paris: Bibliothèque nationale de France, 1994).

Codices Vaticani latini: codices 679–1134

Biblioteca Apostolica Vaticana, *Codices Vaticani latini* (Rome: Typis Polyglottis Vaticanis, 1902–).

Colophons

Bénédictins de Bouveret, *Colophons de manuscrits occidentaux des origines aux xvie siècle*, 6 vols. (Fribourg: Editions universitaires, 1965–79).

De la Mare, *Lyell*

Albinia de la Mare, *Catalogue of the Collection of Medieval Manuscripts Bequeathed to the Bodleian Library, Oxford, by James P.R. Lyell* (Oxford: Clarendon Press, 1971).

DCRB

Descriptive Cataloging of Rare Books, 2nd ed. (Washington, DC: Cataloging Distribution Service, Library of Congress, 1991).

Dutschke, *Huntington Library*

C.W. Dutschke, *Guide to Medieval and Renaissance Manuscripts in the Huntington Library*, 2 vols. (San Marino, Calif.: Huntington Library, 1989).

Dutschke and Rouse, *Claremont Libraries*	C.W. Dutschke and R.H. Rouse, *Medieval and Renaissance Manuscripts in the Claremont Libraries*, Medieval and Renaissance Manuscripts in California Libraries, 1, University of California Publications: Catalogs and Bibliographies, 3 (Berkeley: University of California Press, 1986).
Ker, *MMBL*	N.R. Ker, *Medieval Manuscripts in British Libraries*, 4 vols. (Oxford: Clarendon Press, 1969–92).
Lieftinck and Gumbert, *Manuscrits dans les Pays-Bas*	G. I. Lieftinck and J. P. Gumbert, *Manuscrits datés conservés dans les Pays-Bas: Catalogue paléographique des manuscrits en écriture latine portant des indications de date*, 2 vols. (Amsterdam: North Holland Press, 1969–1988).
Mynors and Thomson, *Hereford Cathedral Library*	R.A.B. Mynors and R.M. Thomson, *Catalogue of the Manuscripts of Hereford Cathedral Library* (Cambridge: D.S. Brewer, 1993).
Saenger, *Newberry Library*	Paul Saenger, *A Catalogue of the Pre-1500 Western Manuscript Books at the Newberry Library* (Chicago: Chicago University Press, 1989).
Samaran and Marichal, *Manuscrits en écriture latine*	Charles Samaran and Robert Marichal, *Catalogue des manuscrits en écriture latine portant des indications de date, de lieu ou de copiste* (Paris: C.N.R.S., 1959–).
Shailor, *Beinecke Library*	Barbara A. Shailor, *Catalogue of Medieval and Renaissance Manuscripts in the Beinecke Rare Book and Manuscript Library, Yale University*, 3 vols., Medieval & Renaissance Texts and Studies, 34, 48, 100 (Binghamton, N.Y.: Medieval & Renaissance Texts and Studies, 1984–92)
Stubbs, *Select Charters*	William Stubbs, *Select Charters and other Illustrations of English Constitutional History, from the Earliest Times to the Reign of Edward the First*, 9th ed., rev. (Oxford: Clarendon Press, 1921).
Watson, *British Library*	Andrew G. Watson, *Catalogue of Dated and Datable Manuscripts c.700–1600 in the Department of Manuscripts, The British Library* (London: British Library, 1979).

INTRODUCTION

As an undifferentiated group of materials, manuscripts rest uneasily or not at all in the library catalog. Manuscript descriptions reside more often in finding aids that stand apart from the main library catalog, such as handwritten inventories, card files, printed catalogs, or more recently EAD or other DTD electronic records. Depending on the nature of the material, if an entry is given in the main catalog it will usually be a brief record that refers to fuller information to be found elsewhere. Sometimes this brief reference may be all that exists. The primary reason for the general absence of manuscripts from the catalog is because manuscripts exist in such a variety of diverse and complex physical and bibliographical structures and because the depth of information required to identify and describe them is so great that it becomes difficult to provide satisfactory intellectual control over these materials within a single integrated library catalog. The result is that information on manuscripts becomes widely scattered and simply locating this information itself often involves considerable research.

In broad terms, manuscripts are categorized as either literary or archival, and this distinction influences the type of intellectual control that is applied to them: literary manuscripts, because of their individual importance, are generally given item-level cataloging and are subject to bibliographic control, while archival manuscripts, whose importance lies in their aggregate rather than in themselves as individual items, are generally given collection-level cataloging and are subject to archival control. The guidelines customarily used for cataloging manuscripts according to these categories are—for item-level bibliographic control—*Anglo-American Cataloguing Rules*, 2nd ed., revised (Chicago: American Library Association, 1998), chapter 4, and—for collection-level archival control—Stephen Hensen, *Archives, Personal Papers, and Manuscripts: A Cataloging Manual for Archival Repositories, Historical Societies, and Manuscript Libraries*, 2nd ed. (Chicago: Society of American Archivists, 1989).

When cataloging pre-modern manuscripts, however—that is, manuscripts generally produced before the middle of the seventeenth century—these broad categories become less useful, as do the descriptive guidelines that serve them. Both these categories and cataloging guidelines are based on modern notions of manuscripts that do not accord well with the status of pre-modern manuscripts. Both modern and pre-modern archival manuscripts are made up of institutional or personal legal documents, records, reflections, notes, letters, etc. Modern archival manuscripts are best understood in terms of their provenance and the contextual relationships of individual items between one another and within the archive as a whole. In the context of a MARC-based library catalog such materials are most effectively served by collection-level description. Pre-modern archival manuscripts, too, demand the same *respect des fonds*. However, pre-modern manuscripts are more frequently the objects of individual codicological or diplomatic analysis and are, thus, better served by item-level cataloging.

For literary manuscripts, differences in the manner in which modern and pre-modern manuscripts are regarded and cataloged are more complex. Modern literary manuscripts consist largely of authors' rough drafts or finished copies of works that are intended ultimately to appear in print for public consumption. They are earlier incarnations of works whose value lies in the evidence they offer of the creative process, both literary and physical. In so far as they are considered to be "books," this is only in the abstract sense of the works they embody, not the marriage of work and printed object that is the final published product more commonly associated with the term "book." But before the advent of printing in the West in the middle of the fifteenth century, all books were manuscripts. Indeed, scribal methods of production persisted and manuscript books continued to be produced and published, though on a greatly diminished scale, up through the middle of the seventeenth century.[3] These manuscripts were not rough drafts, but finished products, and their physical and bibliographical structures have far more in common with printed books than they do with modern literary manuscripts.

These different characteristics of pre-modern manuscripts call for a more historically informed approach to their cataloging, an approach that redresses the absence of manuscripts in the library catalog and, thus, facilitates readier access to information on them. Both *APPM* and *AACR2R* are premised on a modern notion of manuscripts that, as has been shown above, is not applicable to older materials. *APPM* refers the reader for "certain pre-1600 manuscripts," and "book-like manuscripts (*e.g.*, literary manuscripts and codices) and other manuscript material for which a more bibliographically oriented description may be desirable" to *AACR2R*, chapter 4.[4] However, *AACR2R*, chapter 4, reduces all manuscripts to a single cataloging format on the general principal that they are all "unpublished materials," lacking the usual identifying marks of authorship and publication that distinguish printed books.[5] Even though some additional accommodation is made in *AACR2R* 4.7B23 to record certain special features of "ancient, medieval, and Renaissance manuscripts," *AACR2R* provides insufficient analysis and intellectual control over pre-modern manuscript materials. *Descriptive Cataloging of Ancient, Medieval, Renaissance, and Early modern Manuscripts* (AMREMM) is intended as a supplement to *AACR2R*, chapter 4, in order to provide the level of analysis and intellectual control that these materials require. AMREMM offers guidance for the construction of bibliographic records within a library catalog for manuscripts dating from Antiquity, through the Middle Ages, the Renaissance, and up into the early modern period, in whatever form they may survive (from fragments and loose leaves to single- and multiple-sheet letters, legal documents, and archival records to rolls and bound codices), providing item-level, bibliographic control over both literary and archival manuscripts which—owing to their special historical, artistic, or literary value—require more precise and detailed identification and access than is generally accorded to such materials by *AACR2R* or *APPM*.

---

3. On the later tradition of manuscript production, see, *e.g.*, Peter Beal, *In Praise of Scribes: Manuscripts and their Makers in Seventeenth-Century England* (Oxford: Clarendon Press, 1998); H.R. Woudhuysen, *Sir Philip Sidney and the Circulation of Manuscripts, 1558–1640* (Oxford: Clarendon Press, 1996), 1–203; and Harold Love, *Scribal Publication in Seventeenth-Century England* (Oxford: Clarendon Press, 1993). The standard statement of the outlines of print culture and its departure from scribal culture is Elizabeth L. Eisenstein, *The Printing Press as an Agent of Change: Communications and Cultural Transformations in Early-Modern Europe*, 2 vols. (Cambridge: Cambridge University Press, 1979), I:3–159. Among the various responses to Eisenstein, see in particular Richard H. Rouse, "Backgrounds to Print: Aspects of the Manuscript Book in Northern Europe of the Fifteenth Century," in Mary A. and Richard H. Rouse, *Authentic Witnesses: Approaches to Medieval Texts and Manuscripts*, Publications in Medieval Studies, 17 (Notre Dame: University of Notre Dame Press, 1991), 449–66, which argues for a highly sophisticated, commercial scribal production and publication process before the age of print.

4. *APPM*, p. 9 and n. 2.

5. See *AACR2R* 0.26, 1.4B1, 1.4C8, 1.4D9, 1.4F9; also *APPM* 0.11; and *APPM*, 1st ed. (Washington, D.C., 1983), 2–3.

Over the past two decades substantial advances have been made in cataloging the major collections of medieval and Renaissance manuscripts held in the United States.[6] Most of the major libraries in possession of significant collections of these materials have now issued, or are in the process of issuing, comprehensive printed catalogs of their holdings. These efforts supersede in both technical detail and coverage the earlier surveys carried out by Seymour de Ricci, *Census of Medieval and Renaissance Manuscripts in the United States and Canada*, 3 vols. (New York, 1935–40), and by C.U. Faye and W.H. Bond, *Supplement to the Census of Medieval and Renaissance Manuscripts in the United States and Canada* (New York, 1962) which, until the relatively recent publication of these comprehensive catalogs, served largely as the standard means of access to these collections. These recent efforts represent a methodological consensus which the present cataloging rules take as their basis. Implemented in MARC 21, the result is a combination of bibliographic control and electronic format that enables manuscript catalog records created according to *AMREMM* to be integrated into any library's on-line public access catalog. It is hoped that contribution of these records to the national bibliographic databases will also eventually create an electronic union catalog for ancient, medieval, Renaissance, and early modern manuscripts that will eventually encompass not only the holdings of North American libraries but those of other countries as well.

---

6. A review of the major cataloging efforts in the United States over the past twenty years is given in the preface to Mirella Ferrari, *Medieval and Renaissance Manuscripts at the University of California, Los Angeles*, ed. R.H. Rouse, Medieval and Renaissance Manuscripts in California Libraries, 2, University of California Publications: Catalogs and Bibliographies, 7 (Berkeley: University of California Press, 1991), xi–xvii. See also Gregory A. Pass, "Electrifying Research in Medieval and Renaissance Manuscripts," *Papers of the Bibliographical Society of America* 94 (2000): 507–30.

0. GENERAL RULES

Contents

0A. SCOPE

These guidelines are intended to apply to all manuscript materials ranging in date from late Antiquity through the Middle Ages and the Renaissance and up into the early modern period. Although the year 1600 is generally considered an effective terminal date for scribal or manuscript production of books, manuscript book production and publication continue in varying degrees well into the seventeenth century and for some categories of materials even later. The application of these guidelines, therefore, should be governed more by the nature of the material and its method of production than by any arbitrary chronological limit.

These guidelines are intended primarily for Latin and Western European vernacular manuscripts, though it is hoped that the directions for description and the categories of information outlined especially in the notes will be found broad enough to accommodate manuscripts from other traditions as well, such as Greek, Hebrew, Coptic, Ethiopic, Arabic, etc. They may be applied to literary manuscripts, letters, legal documents, and archival records whether these materials are in the form of fragments, single leaves or sheets, rolls, or bound or unbound manuscript codices containing one or multiple works, regardless of whether these materials have been written, drawn, or painted on parchment, paper, papyrus, or other media.

A manuscript is understood in the literal sense here to mean any item written by hand (*manu scriptus*). This definition, therefore, excludes such items as typescripts, mimeographs, or other mechanical or electronic means of substitution for handwriting customarily included in the manuscripts format. These guidelines may also be applied to reproductions of manuscripts in microform, photographic, or electronic formats. However, they are not for use in cataloging published facsimile editions of manuscripts.

These guidelines conform to *Anglo-American Cataloguing Rules*, 2nd ed., rev. (1998), which are to be followed in default of any specific provision otherwise given here. Other cataloging rules, such as *Descriptive Cataloging of Rare Books*, 2nd ed. (1991) or Stephen L. Henson, *Archives, Personal Papers, and Manuscripts*, 2nd ed. (1989), may be used as supplements in cases where the provisions given in those guides prove more appropriate to a particular item.

An experienced manuscripts cataloger will find a great deal more information to incorporate into a manuscript description than can be addressed even in specialized rules such as these, or than may be appropriate for inclusion in a library catalog. Every manuscript is unique, and there are certain to be instances when directions given here will not suffice. The purpose of these guidelines is not to limit the necessarily interpretive role of the manuscripts cataloger, but simply to establish a common framework within which a manuscript catalog description can be constructed.

0B. Sources of information

0B1. Chief source of information

The chief source of information for any manuscript is the manuscript itself, consisting of those parts of the manuscript that are written in a script or hand *contemporary* with—though not necessarily identical to—the script or hand of the main body of text of the manuscript. Information is to be preferred from a title page or colophon, if either is present. In the case of letters, legal documents, and archival records, the protocol or eschatocol is to be preferred.[7]

In the absence of a title page or colophon, information is to be transcribed or obtained wherever it may be found in its fullest form within the manuscript in one of the following sources generally in this order of preference:

- Opening or closing rubric
- Running title

---

7. For a general introduction to the structure of medieval documents and documentary criticism, see Leonard E. Boyle, "Diplomatics," in *Medieval Studies: An Introduction*, ed. James M. Powell, 2nd ed. (Syracuse, N.Y.: Syracuse University Press, 1992), 82–113. For detailed subject and bibliographic orientation, see Olivier Guyotjeannin, Jacques Pycke, and Benoît-Michel Tock, *Diplomatique médiévale*, L'Atelier du médiéviste, 2 (Turnhout: Brepols, 1993).

- Contents list
- Incipit
- Explicit
- Other evidence, *e.g.*, script, decoration, layout, binding, etc.

If no satisfactory information is available from within the manuscript, information is to be transcribed or obtained wherever it may be found in its fullest form on an original binding written in a script or hand contemporary with—though not necessarily identical to—the script or hand of the main body of text of the manuscript, appearing on the cover, spine, or fore-edge, or in the case of letters, legal documents, and archival records, the dorse. For manuscript corrections made in a contemporary or later script or hand, see 0F6.

If no satisfactory contemporary information is available from any of these sources, transcribe or obtain it from one of the following *later* alternate sources of information generally in this order of preference and enclose it in square brackets:

- Title page, colophon, rubrics, running titles, contents list, incipits or explicits within the manuscript written in a script or hand *later than* the script or hand of the main body of text of the manuscript
- Cover, spine, or fore-edge title on an original or later binding, or in the case of legal documents or letters, the dorse, written in a script or hand *later than* the script or hand of the main body of text of the manuscript
- Published or unpublished descriptions of the item emanating from or recognized as authoritative by the holding institution (*e.g.*, catalogs)
- A published edition or study of the item.
- Other reference sources

The absence of square brackets indicates that information is present in a manuscript and is contemporary or original (*i.e.*, taken from the chief source of information). The use of square brackets indicates that information is either present in a manuscript and contemporary or original, but supplemented by the cataloger, as in the expansion of abbreviations (*i.e.*, taken from the chief source of information); or present in a manuscript, but of a later date (*i.e.*, taken from an alternate source of information); or not present in a manuscript at all, but taken from some other alternate source of information. Regardless of whether information is taken from the chief source or an alternate source of information, indicate in a note the specific source and location within the manuscript from which information is obtained. Indicate in a note also if the information is in a script or hand *later than* the main body of text of the manuscript.

0B1.1 *Optional*

If a published catalog description emanating from or recognized as authoritative by the holding institution already exists for a manuscript, use this alternate source of information as a substitute for the chief source of information. In areas where information is normally transcribed from the chief source of information, instead take this information from the alternate source and enclose it in square brackets, eliminating any marks of editorial intervention that may have been used in this alternate source of information. Indicate in a note the source of this alternate information (see 7B1, 7B3, 7B27). If information from this alternate source is augmented or corrected by comparison to the chief source of information, indicate this in a note.

0B2. Prescribed sources of information

The prescribed source(s) of information for each area of the description of a manuscript is set out below.

Area	Prescribed source of information
Title and statement of responsibility	Chief source of information
Edition / Version	Chief source of information
Production, Date, etc.	Chief source of information
Physical Description	The entire item
Notes	Any source

Enclose in square brackets information transcribed or obtained from sources other than the prescribed source of information.

0C. Punctuation

The system employed for encoding information (MARC, EAD, typed cards, etc.) will determine the applicability of some or all of the following rules for prescribed punctuation in the catalog record. See also 0F for special rules on transcription and editorial practice when transcribing source text.

Precede each area, other than the first, by a full stop, space, dash, space (. –), unless the area begins a new paragraph.

Precede or enclose each occurrence of an element of an area with the standard punctuation prescribed at the head of each chapter in these rules for that area.

Precede and follow each mark of prescribed punctuation by a space, except for the comma, full stop, opening and closing parentheses, and opening and closing square brackets. The comma, full stop, and closing parenthesis and square bracket are not preceded by a space; the opening parenthesis and square bracket are not followed by a space.

Precede the first element of each area, other than the first element of the first area or the first element of an area beginning a new paragraph, by a full stop, space, dash, space. When that element is not present in a description, precede the first element that is present by a full stop, space, dash, space instead of the prescribed punctuation for that element.

Follow conventions of modern punctuation when transcribing information from the source, adding mandatory ISBD marks of punctuation where applicable. Since information is transcribed in a regularized form (see 0F1, 0F3), do not reproduce original punctuation that would be contrary to modern conventions of punctuation or that would result in double punctuation.[8]

> Transcription:
> A dynner provided in the treasourye chamber for the lord treasourer, the barons, and other officers of theschequire, sitting there uppon hir maiesties affaires : the nynthe daie of December in the xxxth yeare of hir highnes most prosperous reign et anno domini 1587
>
> (**Source, at head of page:** *A Dynner provided in the Treasourye chamber for the Lord Treasourer the Barons and other Officers of theschequire, sitting there vppon hir Maiesties affaires: the nynthe daie of December in the xxxth yeare of hir highnes most prosperous Reign Et Anno Domini 1587*)
> [Dawson and Kennedy-Skipton, *Elizabethan Handwriting, no. 19*]

Indicate an interpolation (*i.e.*, data taken from outside a prescribed source of information) by enclosing it in square brackets. Indicate a conjectural interpolation by adding a question mark following the data within the square brackets. Indicate the omission of part of an element by the mark of omission; precede and follow the mark of omission by a space (...). Indicate lacunae by enclosing the mark of omission within square brackets ([...]). Omit any area, element of an area, or extraneous information that does not apply in describing an item (see 1A2); also omit its prescribed or enclosing punctuation. Do not indicate the omission of an area or element of an area by the mark of omission.

When adjacent elements within one area are to be enclosed in square brackets, generally enclose them in a single set of square brackets. However, when these interpolations arise from correction, expansion of abbreviation, or supplementing faulty text (see 0F5–6, 0F8), use separate pairs of brackets for each occurrence. When adjacent elements are in separate areas, enclose each element in a set of square brackets.

When an element ends with an abbreviation followed by a full stop or ends with a mark of omission and the punctuation following that element either is or begins with a full stop, omit the full stop that constitutes or begins the prescribed punctuation.

If the source includes the punctuation marks ... or [ ], replace them by — and ( ), respectively.

0D. LEVELS OF DETAIL IN THE DESCRIPTION
Two levels of detail in the description are available:

- Summary
- Detailed

---

8. For a concise introduction to punctuation in the Middle Ages, see Bernhard Bischoff, *Latin Palaeography: Antiquity and the Middle Ages*, trans. Dáibhí Ó Cróinín and David Ganz (Cambridge: Cambridge University Press, 1990), 169–73. A more detailed account is given by M.B. Parkes, *Pause and Effect: An Introduction to the History of Punctuation in the West* (Berkeley: University of California Press, 1993).

Both levels of detail in the description share the same basic set of elements and differ from one another most significantly in the depth of treatment in the notes (see 7A3)—particularly in the contents note (see 7B5), the amount of required added entry access (see Appendix A3), and whether separate analysis is given to multiple works contained in an item (see Appendix B).

Summary description is intended primarily to give ready access to the work or works contained in a manuscript, while also giving some account of the essential physical features of the item. This level of description differs from detailed description in the abbreviated treatment given to material in the notes (see 7A4)—particularly in the contents note where the usual sequence of opening rubric, incipit, explicit, and closing rubric of the work or works contained in an item is generally not transcribed in favor of briefer supplied or uniform titles (see 7B5.1.1). Required added entry access is limited to place of production and the uniform title of the manuscript (see Appendix A3.1). Separate analytic treatment of multiple works contained in an item may be given if desired.

Detailed description is intended to give fuller notice to both textual and paleographical, codicological, artistic, and other physical features of a manuscript. Separate analytic treatment of multiple works contained in an item is required for detailed description when applicable (see Appendix B). A detailed description is distinguished primarily by the transcription of the sequence of opening rubric, incipit, explicit, and closing rubric of the work or works contained in an item (see 7B5.1.1) and by fuller information given in the notes describing textual and physical features (see 7A3.2), particularly the inclusion of a collation statement (see 7B7). Detailed description is flexible in terms of the overall extent of information that it may contain in the notes. While certain categories of information are required in a detailed description and while it may accommodate and certainly imply the possibility of a greater wealth of information than a summary description, the actual extent and detail with which information is conveyed beyond minimum requirements is determined by the cataloging agency.

The following basic set of elements must be included in all manuscript catalog records, regardless of the level of detail in the description, if applicable and available:

1. Title and statement of responsibility
    Title proper
    Parallel title
    Other title information
    First and subsequent statements of responsibility
2. Edition / Version
    Statement of edition / version
    Statement of responsibility relating to edition / version
4. Place and date of production
5. Physical description
    Extent
    Other physical details
    Dimensions
7. Notes

0E. LANGUAGE AND SCRIPT OF THE DESCRIPTION

Give information in the language and system of script (*e.g.*, Roman, Greek, Hebrew, Arabic, or other) of the source—as available typographic facilities permit—whenever text is transcribed from the source for the following areas:

- Title and statement of responsibility
- Edition / version

Provide interpolations enclosed in square brackets using the language and system of script of the source when supplying missing or effaced text or when expanding abbreviations. Replace symbols (*e.g.*, a notary's sign manual) that cannot be reproduced by available typographic facilities with a cataloger's description in square brackets in the language of the cataloging agency. Render all other elements of the description in the language of the cataloging agency, except when transcribing text in a note.

0F. TRANSCRIPTION AND EDITORIAL PRACTICE

The following section provides a general guide for transcribing and editing manuscript source text for use in the catalog record. Diverse transcription and editorial practices exist and several of these may be employed at the same time in a single catalog record depending upon the purpose the transcribed text serves. A general transcription and editorial practice is established here for use in the title and statement of responsibility area and in the edition/version area. This general practice may also be used for transcribing and editing source text in the notes, or a more detailed transcription method may be adopted for use, depending upon the policy of the cataloging institution.

Transcription of manuscript text differs in many respects from transcription of printed text and these differences have important epistemological and practical consequences for the information contained in the catalog record. A basic principle of cataloging printed texts is that information is transcribed as accurately as possible as it is found in the chief source of information.[9] Incunabula and early-printed texts often present difficulty in this regard because of the wide variety of irregular spellings, punctuation, capitalization, and use of abbreviation they possess. Manuscript texts, however, exhibit these qualities to a much higher degree, particularly in the use of abbreviation, which makes their transcription especially challenging—all the more so when it is further taken into consideration that the process involves transferring information from a handwritten source into a typographic medium. Because of differences between graphic (*i.e.*, written) and typographic (*i.e.*, printed) letter forms, transcription of manuscript text is not a straightforward process of transliteration, but frequently requires numerous editorial decisions to be made. Consequently, the role of the cataloger in transcribing manuscript text is best conceived of as interpretation, whereas in the case of printed texts it is usually understood to be literal transcription. The final typographic representation of manuscript text, then, is necessarily a subjective matter and the manuscript catalog record, even at the level of transcription, is understood to be interpretive.[10]

---

9. See *AACR2R* 1.0F, 1.1B1, 2.14E; *DCRB* 0E–0J, Appendix B.

10. See, *e.g.*, the statement of editorial principles in Dawson and Kennedy-Skipton, *Elizabethan Handwriting*, 22–24; also *APPM*, 1st ed., 3.

As a practical consideration, it should also be appreciated that while a work may exist in multiple copies, each manuscript copy of its text is a unique manifestation, and that while titles given to a work may be the same across multiple manuscript copies, they may differ in their spelling or degree of abbreviation, or they may be entirely unalike. Effectively each title is unique, although the work is the same. Access, then, to a work via transcribed title is not an efficient means either of retrieving a single manifestation or as a means of collocating multiple manifestations, unless the researcher already knows the particular form of the transcribed title being sought. Much more effective as a means of retrieval is access through uniform title for the work or through the uniform title of the manuscript itself. The methods of transcription discussed below take into account the mediated nature of manuscript transcription and are intended to eliminate, or at least to diminish, the need for additional access points giving multiple typographic variations of transcribed manuscript text.

0F1. Methods of transcription

The methods of transcription required or available for use in the catalog record differ from one another in regard to the extent that they regularize or preserve aspects of source text such as original spelling, punctuation, and pre-modern letter forms. The choice of transcription method is guided by the purpose the transcribed text serves within the catalog record.

A method of transcription is defined below (see 0F2–0F8) that is required for use when transcribing source text in the title and statement of responsibility area. This method prescribes, among other things, that pre-modern letter forms be regularized to accord with modern conventions (see 0F2), that pre-modern or irregular punctuation and word division also be regularized to accord with modern conventions (see 0F3–0F4), but that pre-modern or irregular spellings found in the source be maintained (see 0F5).

Any method of transcription determined appropriate by the cataloging agency is permissible in the notes, so long as that method is a clear and consistent one. It is recommended that the method defined for use in the title and statement of responsibility area also be applied in the notes, although abbreviations may be expanded silently in order to provide a more easily readable text. Alternatively, if it is desirable to record certain characteristics of the text, such as original punctuation or additions, suppressions, or substitutions to the text, a cataloging agency may choose to employ a semi-diplomatic method of transcription (see 7A2).

0F2. Letter forms

0F2.1

In general, transcribe pre-modern letter forms using their modern equivalents, but maintain language-specific characters, such as Anglo-Saxon ð and þ. Transcribe ligatures by giving their component parts as separate letters. The ligature e-caudata (ę, e-cedilla, e *cédillé*, hooked- or looped-e) should similarly be rendered by separating its component parts into a and e. Do not, however, separate the component letters of the ligatured digraphs æ in Anglo-Saxon, œ in French, or æ and œ in Scandinavian languages. Do not reproduce or distinguish between varying graphic forms of letters.

0F2.2

Follow the conventions given below for resolving transcription of the letter forms short-**i**, **i**-*longa*, **u**, and **v** in Latin and vernacular texts. The use of these different letter forms in the source text is conditioned variously by the conventions of the script, the consistency or individual practice of the scribe, the position of these letters within a word, and the language itself.

The purpose of these conventions is simply to provide a consistent and easily readable transcription, not to provide a faithful typographic representation of the graphic letter forms used in the source. Transcription that more accurately reflects graphic letter forms used in the source text may be given in the notes.

a) short-**i** / **i**-*longa*[11]

Latin texts

For Latin texts, transcribe both of the letter forms short-**i** and **i**-*longa* (usually represented in print as **j**) as either minuscule or majuscule **i/I**, depending upon context, without exception. The use in the source of differing graphic forms of the same letter (**i**) does not in itself imply vocalic or consonantal value, though the phonetic value of **i** does change depending upon its position. The **i**-*longa* is a characteristic feature of cursive documentary scripts. In its minuscule form, it appears usually in initial or final position, though it will occasionally be found in medial position as well. It is also commonly found in combination with short-**i** to distinguish the two minims, as frequently in the case of roman numerals. Its appearance in formal book scripts, however, is unusual and generally discouraged. Short-**i** is used in formal book scripts throughout the Middle Ages, though **i**-*longa* is common from the end of the thirteenth century as an element of formalized cursive documentary scripts adapted as book scripts. In majuscule form, whether in cursive documentary or book scripts both short-**i** and **i**-*longa* resemble various forms of the modern upper-case **J**, but similarly there is no vocalic or consonantal value implied in its use. In no instance should short-**i** or **i**-*longa*, whether in minuscule or majuscule form, be transcribed as the modern letter **j/J** to indicate vocalic or consonantal value.

> *E.g.*, transcribe:
>
> | | | |
> |---|---|---|
> | xii̇ Februarii̇ | *as* | xii Februarii |
> | ei̇us | *as* | eius |
> | i̇udex | *as* | iudex |
> | i̇US | *as* | Ius *or* ius |
> | i̇tem / i̇tem | *as* | Item *or* item |
> | i̇ohannes | *as* | Iohannes |

---

11. For accounts of the use of short-**i** and **i**-*longa*, see, *e.g.*, E.A. Lowe, "Studia palaeographica," in *Palaeographical Papers, 1907–1965*, ed. Ludwig Bieler, 2 vols. (Oxford: Clarendon Press, 1972), I:2–65, and *The Beneventan Script: A History of the South Italian Minuscule* (Oxford: Clarendon Press, 1914), 136, 300–13; Charles Johnson and Hilary Jenkinson, *English Court Hand, A.D. 1066 to 1500*, 2 vols. (Oxford: Clarendon Press, 1915), I:24–26; Hilary Jenkinson, *The Later Court Hands in England from the Fifteenth to the Seventeenth Century* (Cambridge: Cambridge University Press, 1927; rpt. New York: Ungar, 1969), 36; Dawson and Kennedy-Skipton, *Elizabethan Handwriting*, 14.

Vernacular texts

For vernacular texts, transcribe the letter forms short-**i** and **j**-*longa* as minuscule or majuscule **i/I** or **j/ J** according to their vocalic or consonantal values. However, where a text employs a short-**i** where **j**-*longa* would be expected, maintain this usage.

E.g., transcribe:

	įci / įci	*as*	Ici *or* ici
	la įustice	*as*	la justice
	įehan	*as*	Jehan
	įsabeau	*as*	Isabeau
	įudgement / įudgement	*as*	Judgement *or* judgement
	įohn	*as*	John
	įndenture / įndenture	*as*	Indenture *or* indenture
but			
	tousįours	*as*	tousiours (*not as* tousjours)
	įustifyed	*as*	iustifyed (*not as* justifyed)

b) u / v[12]

Latin texts

For Latin texts, transcribe the letter forms **u** and **v** according to their modern vocalic or consonantal values in either minuscule or majuscule form depending upon context. The use in the source of **u** and **v** as differing graphic forms of the same letter (**u**) does not itself imply vocalic or consonantal value, though the phonetic value of u does change depending upon position. In minuscule form, the letter **u** appears in initial, medial, and final positions in book scripts and cursive scripts throughout the early Middle Ages. The **v**-shaped **u**, or letter **v**, appears from the twelfth century in cursive documentary scripts where it occurs more frequently in initial position, with **u** in medial or final position, and from the thirteenth century in formal cursive documentary scripts adapted as book scripts. Otherwise, book scripts in the later Middle Ages more frequently employ the letter **u** in initial position, though **v**-shaped **u** can be found as well. In majuscule form, the **v**-shaped **u** is used throughout the Middle Ages, though **u** is also found. Similarly, there is no vocalic or consonantal value implied by the letter form itself.

E.g., transcribe:

seruus	*as*	servus
uir	*as*	vir
vt	*as*	ut
VTRVM	*as*	utrum
VIRTVS	*as*	virtus

---

12. For accounts of the use of **u** and **v**, see H. Maxwell Lyte, "'U' and 'V': A Note on Palaeography," *Bulletin of the Institute of Historical Research* 2 (1924–25): 63–65; Johnson and Jenkinson, *English Court Hand*, I:49–51; Jenkinson, *Later Court Hands*, 38–39; Dawson and Kennedy-Skipton, *Elizabethan Handwriting,*, 15–16.

Vernacular texts

For vernacular texts, transcribe the letter forms **u**, **v**, and **vv** as minuscule or majuscule **u/U** or **v/V** or **w/W**, according to their vocalic or consonantal value.

E.g., transcribe:

vsage	*as*	usage
sauueur	*as*	sauveur
vppon	*as*	uppon
gouernaunce	*as*	governaunce
VNIVERSALL	*as*	universall
VVilliam	*as*	William

0F3. Capitalization, accents, and other diacritical marks

Follow the rules for capitalization given in *AACR2R* Appendix A. Do not reproduce original capitalization from the source that would be contrary to modern conventions of capitalization. Do not add accents or other diacritical marks not found in the source.

0F4. Word division, syllable separation, and line fillers

Introduce word division as necessary when transcribing text that does not clearly distinguish between individual words. Transcribe syllables of a word that are separated within a line or between lines of text as a single word without indicating the discontinuity, regardless of whether the source signals the separation (usually by a single or double stroke). Do not transcribe or otherwise attempt to represent line fillers. Do not indicate line divisions within a text or breaks across a page.

E.g., transcribe:

ARMAVIRUMQUECANO	*as*	Arma virumque cano
deanima	*as*	de anima
aeta | tis	*as*	aetatis
incar//nationem	*as*	incarnationem

0F5. Variantly and erroneously spelled words

Transcribe variantly and erroneously spelled words as they appear in the source. Do not correct or normalize spellings that follow pre-modern orthographic conventions or that are merely erratically or poorly spelled. Maintain variant spelling conventions favored by the source (*e.g.*, c/t, y/i, e/ae) when transcribing text and expanding abbreviations. If a misspelling consists of simply the omission of a letter, supply the missing letter in square brackets. If a word is spelled, declined, or conjugated in a manner clearly owing to error, ignorance, or regional practice—that is, it does not simply use a non-classical spelling—signal this irregularity by the use of "[sic]."

admonicio / admonitio
paradysus / paradisus
celum / caelum
miser[i]cordia

> Decretorum descordantium [sic] concordia (*for discordantium*)
> dissipuli [sic] (*for discipuli*)
> vinum est mera [sic] (*for merum*)

0F6. Missing letters and illegible text

If the space for an enlarged or otherwise decorated or illuminated initial letter has been left blank and no guide letter is present, supply the missing letter enclosed in square brackets. If a guide letter is present, supply the missing letter, but do not enclose it in square brackets. If other letters or text are illegible or missing from the manuscript owing to damage or trimming, supply the missing letters or text in square brackets. If the original reading cannot be recovered, or if at least a conjectural reading cannot be supplied, substitute a hyphen for each of the missing characters and enclose it in square brackets. If the number of missing characters cannot be determined, substitute the mark of omission. Provide a note indicating the nature of such omissions or damage.

> [I]n principio
> stip[-----]s
> [...]ter

0F7. Manuscript corrections

If a text possesses corrections arising from additions, suppressions, or substitutions (*e.g.,* marginal or interlinear insertion, cancellation by erasure, strikethrough, expunctuation, transformation, or superimposition) in a script or hand contemporary with—though not necessarily identical to—the script or hand of the main body of text of the manuscript, incorporate these corrections into the transcription of the text without signal. If the correcting script or hand is later than the script or hand of the main body of text of the manuscript, transcribe the original text as it appears in the source without incorporating any of the corrections. If desired, transcribe the text in a note using a semi-diplomatic transcription to show the state of correction. If there is doubt whether the correcting script or hand is contemporary, transcribe the uncorrected text.

0F8. Abbreviations[13]

Expand all suspensions, contractions, nomina sacra, Tironian notes, symbols, and other abbreviations to their full form, enclosing supplied letters or words in square brackets. When a choice of spelling is

---

13. The standard manual for medieval abbreviations is Adriano Cappelli, *Lexicon abbreviaturarum: Dizionario di abbreviature latine ed italiane*, 6th ed. (Milan: Ulrico Hoepli, 1967). See also Auguste Pelzer, *Abbréviations latines médiévales: Supplément au Dizionario di abbreviature latine ed italiane de Adriano Cappelli*, 2nd ed. (Louvain: Publications universitaires; Paris: Béatrice-Nauwelaerts, 1966), and the translation of Cappelli's introductory essay, "Brachigrafia medioevale," as *The Elements of Abbreviation in Medieval Latin Paleography*, trans. David Heimann and Richard Kay, Univeirisity of Kansas Publications, Library Series, 47 (Lawrence, Kans.: University of Kansas Libraries, 1982); Charles Trice Martin, *The Record Interpreter*, 2nd ed. (London: Stevens, 1910; rpt. Hildesheim: G. Olms, 1969); W. M. Lindsay, *Notae Latinae: An Account of Abbreviations in Latin MSS. of the Early Minuscule Period (c. 700–850)* (Cambridge: Cambridge University Press, 1915; rpt. Hildesheim: G. Olms, 1963); Ludwig Traube, *Nomina sacra: Versuch einer Geschichte der christlichen Kurzung* (Munich: C.H. Beck, 1907). A concise and systematic introduction is given by Bischoff, *Latin Palaeography*, 150–68, and a non-specialist introduction by L.C. Hector, *The Handwriting of English Documents*, 2nd ed. (London: Edward Arnold, 1966), 29–39.

available in expanding abbreviations, render the expansion in accordance with the spelling conventions used in the text if it is possible to determine them with any consistency. In other words, do not substitute a classical spelling where the manuscript would use a medieval spelling (*e.g.*, do not substitute "prae" where the source favors "pre"). Do not reproduce Tironian notae, the ampersand, or other symbols, but instead supply in square brackets the letters or words for which they stand in the language of the text. Transcribe each expansion or supplied word in its own set of square brackets (*e.g.*, "… p[re]d[ict]or[um] [et] …").

E.g., transcribe:

&	*as*	[et] *or* [and] *or* …
7	*as*	[et] *or* [and] *or* …
÷	*as*	[est]
dominū	*as*	dominu[m]
grā	*as*	gr[ati]a
v₃	*as*	v[idelicet]

Where the expansion of an abbreviation is conjectural, use a question mark following the supplied letters or words within the square brackets. Where it is unclear how an abbreviation should be expanded, as in certain place names and personal names, use an apostrophe to indicate the presence of a mark of abbreviation, regardless of the actual form of the mark of abbreviation in the source text.

E.g., transcribe:

rō	*as*	r[ati]o[nem?]
Berk'	*as*	Berk'
Ricardus de Hoton'	*as*	Ricardus de Hoton'

Retain abbreviations for ordinal numbers, units of weight, money, and measurement, and customarily abbreviated titles of address.

E.g., transcribe:

xx.	*as*	xx.
xv^th	*as*	xvth
iv^to	*as*	ivto
CC^mo	*as*	CCmo
5s.	*as*	5s.
M^r	*as*	Mr.
K^t	*as*	Kt.

13

1. TITLE AND STATEMENT OF RESPONSIBILITY AREA

Contents

1A. PRELIMINARY RULE

1A1. Punctuation

For instructions on the use of spaces before and after prescribed punctuation, see 0C.

Precede the title of a supplement or section by a full stop.

Precede each parallel title by an equals sign.

Precede each unit of other title information by a colon.

Precede the first statement of responsibility by a diagonal slash.

Precede each subsequent statement of responsibility by a semicolon.

For the punctuation of this area when there is no collective title, see 1B1.4.

On reproducing original punctuation from the source, see 0C, 0F3.

1A2. Sources of information

1A2.1

Take information recorded in this area from the chief source of information. Record in a note the location within the item where this information was obtained. Enclose in square brackets all information taken from alternate sources of information.

1A2.2

Omit from a title or statement of responsibility elements that do not constitute title information or a statement of responsibility. For instance, omit such words as "incipit" or "explicit" that may follow or precede a title or statement of responsibility. Omit other extraneous elements such as pious invocations, epigrams, mottoes, dedications, statements of patronage, etc. Do not use the mark of omission to indicate the exclusion of extraneous elements or other information preceding or following a title or statement of responsibility.

> P[ublii] Vergilii Mar[onis] Bucolicorum liber
>
> (**Source of information, opening rubric:** *P. VIRGILII MAR. BVCOLICORVM LIBER INCIPIT.*)
>
> [Alexander and De la Mare, *Italian Mss.,* 39]

> Speculum iudiciale / a Magistro Guillelmo Duranti compositum
>
> (**Source of information, opening rubric:** *In nomine domini et gloriose virginis matris eius incipit speculum iudiciale a magistro Guillelmo duranti compositum.*)
>
> [Dutschke, *Huntington Library,* II:604]

> Commentariorum C[aii] Iulii Caesaris de bello Gallico liber / Iulius Celsus Consta[n]tinus quintus co[n]sul emendavit
>
> (**Source of information, opening rubric:** *COMMENTARIORVM C. IVLII CAESARIS DE BELLO GALLICO LIBER PRIMVS INCIPIT FOELICITER. IVLIVS CELSVS CONSTA[N]TINVS QVINTVS CO[N]SVL EMENDAVIT.*)
>
> [Alexander and De la Mare, *Italian Mss.,* 131]

Omit from a title the numeration of particular chapters, books, or other significant parts of a work when that work is present in its entirety or in more units than the title would accurately describe. If a work is not present in its entirety, indicate in a note the number of chapters, books, or other significant parts of the work that are present.

> Macrobii Theodosii viri illustrissimi Saturnalium liber

(*Sources of information, opening rubric:* Macrobii theodosii uiri illustrissimi Saturnalium liber primus incipit. **Closing rubric:** Macrobii theodosii viri illustrissimi Co[n]uiuior[um] tertii diei Liber et ultimus explicit . . .)

[Alexander and De la Mare, *Italian Mss.*, 41–43]

1A2.3

If more than one title and statement of responsibility is present for the same work, transcribe the one that is clearly given prominence over any other by its presence on a title page or in a colophon, or one that is distinguished by its type or grade of script, color of ink, or placement on the page, even though it may be shorter than a fuller form of a title and statement of responsibility found elsewhere. In the absence of a title and statement of responsibility distinguished by its presence on a title page or in a colophon, or by its prominence, transcribe the one that may be found in its fullest form. Give variant titles in a note for variations of title and statement of responsibility (see 7B4), if these are not already recorded as part of a contents note.

Modus quomodo parliamentum regis Anglie et Anglorum suorum tenebatur

(*Sources of information, opening rubric:* Hic discribitur modus quomodo parliamentum regis Anglie et anglorum suorum tenebatur. **Closing rubric:** Explicit modus parliamenti.)

[Saenger, *Newberry Library*, 56]

Vita et passio S[ancte] Thome Cantuariensis Archiepiscopi et Martyris

(*Sources of information, opening rubric (preface):* Incipit prefatio in vitam S. Thome Cantuariensis archiepiscopi et martyris. **Opening rubric (text):** In nomine p. et f. et s.s. Willelmus secundus. Incipit Vita S. Thome Cantuariensis archiepiscopi et martyris. **Closing rubric:** Explicit vita et passio S. Thome Cantuariensis archiepiscopi et martyris.)

[De la Mare, *Lyell*, 9–10]

Liber ethicorum / compilatus a Fratre Alberto Theutonico de Ordine Fratrum Predicatorum

(*Sources of information, opening rubric:* Incipit ethica fratris Alberti cuius primus tractatus est de communibus … **Closing rubric:** Explicit liber ethicorum compilatus a fratre alberto theutonico de ordine fratrum predicatorum.)

[Shailor, *Beinecke Library*, III:311]

In selecting between titles, give preference—all other choices being equal—to one that includes a statement of responsibility.

Politicorum Aristotilis liber

(***Sources of information, opening rubric***: *Politicorum Aristotilis liber primus incipit …* ***Closing rubric***: *Explicit liber politicorum deo gracias.*)

[Saenger, Newberry Library, 42]

If the preceding criteria fail to produce a satisfactory title and statement of responsibility, the choice of title and statement of responsibility is at the discretion of the cataloger.

Sancti Ambrosii Episcopi De officiis ministrorum

(***Sources of information, opening rubric***: *Incipit liber I^{us} sancti Ambrosii episcopi de officiis ministrorum.* ***Closing rubric***: *Explicit liber tercius beati Ambrosii de officiis ministrorum.*)

[Saenger, Newberry Library, 25]

Pour se que pluisours gens desirent asavoir la nature des faucons
or
La nature des faucons
or
Des faucons
or
Des oysiaus
or
[Traité de la fauconnerie]

(***Sources of information, incipit***: *Pour se que pluisours gens desirent asavoir la nature des faucons …* ***Explicit***: *Et ce que nous avons dit des oysiaus de proie suffice.* ***Spine title (20th cent.)***: *Traité de la fauconnerie.*)

NB *Possible titles listed in descending order of preference. The full incipit of the work is preferable as the fullest form of the title proper, though the more concise version "La nature des faucons" derived from the incipit is also acceptable. "Des faucons" and "Des oysiaus" are too brief, and "Traité de la fauconnerie," though it is a more apt description of the work, is of a later date than the main body of text. In any case, all versions of the title not selected as the title proper should be recorded in a note and access provided.*

[BnF, Manuscrits, 1983–1992, 93]

1B. Title proper

1B1. Literary and other manuscripts

1B1.1
Transcribe the title proper exactly to wording, order, and spelling, but not necessarily as to punctuation and capitalization. The title proper includes any alternative title, parallel title, other title information, statements of responsibility, or statements of edition/version that either precede or follow the

chief title—if these elements constitute grammatically integral parts of the title proper. Follow the method of transcription as given in 0F. Do not transpose or rearrange information in any way. Expand all abbreviations, punctuate according to modern convention, and capitalize according to the rules given in *AACR2R*, Appendix A.

Le rommant de la rose

Hystoria Brittonum

Actas de las cortes de Madrid año 1393

Regula Sancti Benedicti

Petri Lombardi Sententiarum IV

Sermo Beati Augustini Episcopi de nativitate Domini

Commentarii et expositione Georgii Trapezuntii in aphorismis libri fructus Ptolomei

Transcribe an alternative title as part of the title proper. Precede and follow the word or phrase introducing the alternative title by a comma and capitalize the first word of the alternative title.

Periphyseon, id est, De divisione naturae

Liber physicorum, sive, Auditus physici

Consulta Beati Basilii, que dicuntur, Regula eiusdem

1B1.2
If the only title present on an item is one that has been added subsequent to its creation (that is, absent from the chief source of information, being in a script later than that of the main body of text), record this title in square brackets and provide a note indicating its nature and source. See 0B1.

[Questiones disputate Sancti Thome]

1B1.3
If the title of an item is incorrect or obsolete, and is not simply a variant form of the title, give the correct or current title as the title proper enclosed in square brackets. Transcribe in a note the incorrect or obsolete title information.

1B1.4
If an item containing two or more works lacks a collective title, treat the title of the predominant or most significant work (as determined by the cataloger) as the title proper for the whole item. Follow

this title with the mark of omission and "etc." enclosed in square brackets (… [etc.]) and provide a complete list of the works contained in the item in a contents note, including the work selected as the title proper. Omit any statement of responsibility for the predominant or most significant work that is not a grammatically integral part of the title proper. Give appropriate added entry access (see Appendix A2).

> Carta foreste … [etc.]
>
> (**Sources of information**: *1. fol. 1r–77v: [Title page] [Rubr.] Here begynnethe the Booke named Carta Foreste. 1562. [rubr.]   — 2. fol. 78r–85v: Collection of extracts, in Latin, all concerning laws of forest.*)
>
> [Shailor, *Beinecke Library*, I:127]

> Epistole Ivonis Carnotensis Episcopi … [etc.]
>
> (**Sources of information**: *1. fol. 1r–122v: Incipiunt epistole Iuonis Carnotensis episcopi …—2. fol. 123r–146v: Epistolae ad Amicum / Anon.—3. fol. 147r–154v: Epistolae / Gilbert Foliot— 4. fol. 155r–160v: Vita Sanctae Mariae Egyptiacae / Hildebert of Le Mans …*)
>
> [Mynors and Thomson, *Hereford Cathedral Library*, 72]

1B1.5

If an item containing two or more works lacks a collective title and no single work predominates or the works are of comparable significance , describe the item as a unit. Give the titles of the predominant or most significant works (as determined by the cataloger), treating multiple sources of information as though they were a single source. Separate titles of works by the same author with a space-semicolon-space, and precede titles by different authors, except for the first, with a full stop followed by a single space. Provide a complete list of the works contained in the item in a contents note, including the works selected to describe the item as a unit. Give appropriate added entry access (see Appendix A2). If providing more than a summary description, make in addition a separate description for each significant work.

> Scriptum Ethicorum Aristotelis / secundum Thomam de Aquino. Super libro Rhetoricorum Aristotelis / editum a Fratre Egidio de Roma
>
> (**Sources of information:** *1. fol. 1r–101v,* **opening rubric:** *Scriptum ethicorum aristotelis … secundum Thomam de aquino …— 2. fol. 103r–224r,* **opening rubric:** *Incipit opus super libro rhetoricorum aristotelis. Editum a fratre Egidio de roma …;* **closing rubric:** *Et sic finit sententia super librum rethoricorum aristotelis …*)
>
> [*Codices Vaticani latini: codices 679–1134*, II, i:87]

> Aurelii Augustini Doctoris De sermone Domini in monte ; Sancti Augustini In epistolam Sancti Iohannis Apostoli. Sancti Ambrosii Episcopi De officiis ministrorum

(*Sources of information:* 1. fol. 1r–44v, **opening rubric:** *Aurelii Augustini doctoris de sermone domini in monte liber incipit …*—2. fol. 45r–84v, **opening rubric:** *Incipit tractatus primus sancti Augustini in epistolam sancti Iohannis apostoli ab eo …;* **closing rubric:** *Explicit expositio sancti Augustini super epistolam sancti Iohannis.*— 3. fol. 85r–146r, **opening rubric:** *Incipit liber I^{us} sancti Ambrosii episcopi de officiis ministrorum …;* **closing rubric:** *Explicit liber tercius beati Ambrosii de officiis ministrorum.*)

[Saenger, *Newberry Library*, 25]

If certain works in an item described as a unit do not predominate or are not deemed significant enough to include in the title used to describe the item as a unit, follow this title with the mark of omission and "etc." enclosed in square brackets (… [etc.]).

Hystoria evangelium. Hystoria actuum apostolorum … [etc.]

(*Sources of information:* 1. fol. ir: *Old Testament genealogies*—2. fol. 1r–246r, **incipit:** *Imperatorie maiestatis est in palatio habere mansiones …;* **closing rubric:** *Explicit Hystoria evangelium.*—3. fol. 246r–278v, **opening rubric:** *Incipiunt capitula Hystorie actuum apostolorum …;* **closing rubric:** *Explicit Hystoria actum apostolorum.*)

[Dutschke, *Huntington Library*, II:704–705]

Do not use more than three individually titled works to describe an item as a unit.

1B1.6

If an item lacks a title, supply one as instructed below. Give the source of the supplied title in the note area.

If a work already possesses a title, but no title can be established from the manuscript copy in hand, supply a title in the original language by which the work (other than one written in classical Greek or by a post-classical or Byzantine writer in Greek, or one not otherwise written in a Greek or roman script, as defined in *AACR2R* 25.4B–25.4C) is identified in the following order of preference:

- modern reference sources
- modern printed editions
- early printed editions
- other manuscript copies of the work

[De consolatione philosophiae]

[Historia regum Britanniae]

If a work possesses no title peculiar to itself, supply a brief descriptive title in the language of the cataloging agency—not the language of the work—that reflects the genre and nature of the material.

[Bestiary]

[Herbal]

If the supplied title and the uniform title for the work are the same—as may happen especially in the case of sacred scripture or liturgical works—distinguish the supplied title proper from the uniform title by abridgement or adaptation by emphasizing some particular aspect of the genre or nature of the material.

[Book of hours : use of Rouen]

> **Main entry under:** *Catholic Church*
> **Uniform title:** *Book of hours (Ms. National Art Library. MSL/1902/1654)*
> **Added entry under:** *National Art Library (Great Britain). Manuscript. MSL/1902/1654*

[Psalter]

> **Main entry under:** *Catholic Church*
> **Uniform title:** *Psalter (Ms. Library of Congress. BX2033.A2 1200z)*
> **Added entry under:** *Library of Congress. Manuscript. BX2033.A2 1200z*

[Psalter]

> **Main entry under:** *Catholic Church*
> **Uniform title:** *Psalter (Ms. Utrecht)*
> **Added entry under uniform title:** *Utrecht psalter*

[Acts of the Apostles]

> **Main entry under uniform title:** *Bible. N.T. Acts of the Apostles. Coptic. Pierpont Morgan Library. Manuscript. G.67*
> **Added entry under:** *Pierpont Morgan Library. Manuscript. G.67*

[Apocalypse]

> **Main entry under uniform title:** *Bible. N.T. Revelation. Latin. British Library. Manuscript. Royal 19 B. xv*
> **Added entry under:** *British Library. Manuscript. Royal 19 B. xv*

For standard works accompanied by commentaries or glosses, such as the Bible or the *Corpus iuris civilis* or the *Corpus iuris canonici*, that lack a title—especially when these commentaries or glosses are anonymous or excerpted from other sources—determine which is the primary work, either the text or the commentary or gloss on the text. If the text is primary, supply the title by which the text is commonly known or an abridgement or adaptation of the uniform title of the text emphasizing the presence of accompanying commentary or gloss. If the commentary or gloss is primary (as in the case of a continuous commentary), give the title by which the commentary or gloss is commonly known or the uniform title of the commentary or gloss .

Text primary

[Psalms : with Glossa ordinaria]

> **Main entry under uniform title:** *Bible. O.T. Psalms. Latin. Houghton Library. Manuscript. MS Typ 260*
> **Added entry under uniform title:** *Glossa ordinaria*
> **Added entry under:** *Houghton Library. Manuscript. MS Typ 260*

Commentary primary

[Commentarius in Psalmos]

> **Main entry under:** *Gilbert de La Porré, Bishop, ca. 1075-1154*
> **Uniform title:** *Commentarius in Psalmos*
> **Added entry under uniform title:** *Bible. O.T. Psalms. Latin. Houghton Library. Manuscript. fMS Typ 29*
> **Added entry under:** *Houghton Library. Manuscript. fMS Typ 29*

If none of the provisions for assigning a collective title from disparate individual titles proper within a collection proves satisfactory, supply a uniform or devised title appropriate to the item. If a collection or compilation contains works or items related by theme or genre, supply a title that reflects this theme or genre. For a collection or compilation of literary passages, use the term *florilegium*. For a collection or compilation of passages or items intended for reference, use the term *commonplace book*. For a collection or compilation of materials that are so disparate in nature that they defy classification, use the term *miscellany*.[14] If the items are dated or datable, give the range of dates represented by the content of the collection or compilation as part of the supplied title.

[Treatises on rhetoric]

[Arthurian romances]

[Florilegium]

---

14. For a discussion of the taxonomy of such works as *florilegia*, commonplace books, anthologies, or miscellanies, and of the issues involved in describing them, see Stephen G. Nichols and Siegfried Wenzel, eds., *The Whole Book: Cultural Perspectives on the Medieval Miscellany*, (Ann Arbor: University of Michigan Press, 1996), particularly essays by Siegfried Wenzel, "Sermon Collections and their Taxonomy," 7–21, and Barbara A. Shailor, "A Cataloger's View," 153–67.

[Medical formulary]

[Sermons]

[Commonplace book of legal precedents]

[Year Books, 5–7 Edward III]

[Statuta Nova, 1 Edward III–23 Henry VI]

1B2. Letters, legal documents, and archival records[15]

1B2.1. Content date

Record the date of the content of an item—as opposed to its date of production—as part of the supplied title for letters, legal documents, and archival records. Do not record this information in the place and date of production area. If an item is an original or autograph, assume the content date to be the same as its date of production. Similarly, assume the place of production to be the same. If an item is known to be a later copy and the content date and date of production therefore differ, provide a note indicating the fact of its later date or different place of production.[16]

Give exact dates using Arabic numerals expressed in the form: year, month, day. A wide range of dating systems were employed throughout Western Europe, North Africa, and the Middle East from Antiquity up to the early modern period: the Dionysian or Christian era (*anno domini*), the Jewish era, the Islamic era of the Hegira, the Roman civil calendar, the Christian ecclesiastical calendar, regnal years, legal chronology, and many others. Convert dates given in these or other chronological systems to Arabic numbers and render them according to the Gregorian calendar. Convert all Old Style dates of the Julian calendar (including those prior to 1582) to New Style dates of the Gregorian calendar using January 1 as the beginning of the year.[17] Make any necessary corrections of error. Record original statements of date of production in a note.

---

15. The treatment of the supplied title and the order of its elements set out in this section follows *AACR2R* 4.1B2 where all information in the supplied title is regarded as the title proper. This treatment differs from that given for similar items in *APPM* 1.1B2, 1.1B4–B5, and 1.1E1 where all information following the "form of material" is regarded as other title information.

16. For legal documents that confirm and rehearse the text of an earlier document in full or in part (known as a confirmation, or *vidimus*, or *inspeximus*), catalog the later document.

17. For an introduction to medieval chronology, see R. Dean Ware, "Medieval Chronology," in James M. Powell, ed., *Medieval Studies: An Introduction*, 252–77. For further information on systems of chronology and aids for converting dates, see Reginald Lane Poole, *Medieval Reckonings of Time*, Helps for Students of History, 3 (London: Society for Promoting Christian Knowledge, 1935); C. R. Cheney, *A Handbook of Dates for Students of British History*, rev. ed., Royal Historical Society Guides and Handbooks, 4 (Cambridge: Cambridge University Press, 2000); Guyotjeannin, Pycke, and Tock, *Diplomatique médiévale*, 50–57; E. B. Fryde and F. M. Powicke, *Handbook of British Chronology*, 3rd ed., Royal Historical Society Guides and Handbooks, 2 (London: Royal Historical Society, 1986); A. Giry, *Manuel de diplomatique* (Paris: Hachette, 1893; rpt. Hildesheim: G. Olms, 1972); Adriano Cappelli, *Cronologia, cronografia e calendario perpetuo*, 2nd ed. (Milan: Hoepli, 1930); *AACR2* 22.17A.

1264 Jan. 23
(**Source**: … *in crastino beati Vincentii Martyris, A.D. M*ᵒ*CC*ᵒ*LX*ᵒ*III*ᵒ*, mense Januario.* **N.B.** *year beginning March 1.*)

[Stubbs, *Select Charters*, 397]

1266 Oct. 31
(**Source**: … *pridie kalendas Novembris anno gratiae M*ᵒ*CC*ᵒ*LX*ᵒ*VI*ᵒ*, regni vero domini Henrici regis Angliae anno quinquagesimo primo.*)

[Stubbs, *Select Charters*, 411]

1275 May 19
(**Source**: … *die Dominica in festo Sancti Dunstanii episcopi anno regni eiusdem regis tertio.*)

[Stubbs, *Select Charters*, 444]

1259 Oct. 13
(**Source**: *Anno ab Incarnatione Domini M*ᵒ*CC*ᵒ*L*ᵒ*IX*ᵒ *regni autem Henrici regis, filii regis Johannis, xliii*ᵒ *… in quindena Sancti Michaelis.*)

[Stubbs, *Select Charters*, 390]

1402 Oct. 4
(**Source**: *Millesimo Quadricentessimo secundo. Indiccione decima die iiij*ᵗᵒ *mensis octubris.*)

[Watson, *British Library*, I:29, #31]

1B2.2. Letters

For single letters, supply a title consisting, in the following order, of the form designation *Letter*, the date of writing (expressed as year, month, day), the place of writing, the name of the addressee, and the place to which the letter is addressed, insofar as this information can be ascertained. Enclose the whole title in square brackets, regardless of whether certain elements of the title may or may not be present in the item.

[Letter, 1533 Sept. 26, Waltham Abbey to Arthur Plantagenet, Lord Lisle, Calais]

[Letter, 1454 (?) Feb. 1, Norwich to John Paston I]

For bound or unbound collections of letters lacking a collective title, supply a title consisting of the form designation *Letters* and as many of the title elements given above for a single letter as is consistent with the collection as a whole, but giving at least the inclusive dates for the collection. When appropriate, also include as part of the supplied title bulk dates for the material. Enclose bulk dates in parentheses with the designation *bulk* and following the inclusive dates.

[Letters, 1452–1510]

[Letters, 1555–1635 (bulk 1590–1610)]

1B2.3. Legal documents and archival records

For single legal documents and archival records, such as wills, deeds, charters, mortgages, leases, various manor rolls, warrants, commissions, writs, oaths, etc., supply a title consisting, in the following order, of a word or brief phrase characterizing the type of document, the date of execution (expressed as year, month, day), the name of the principal party or parties involved or to whom the document is directed, and the occasion for the document expressed concisely, insofar as this information can be ascertained. Enclose the whole title in square brackets, regardless of whether certain elements of the title may or may not be present in the item.

> [Grant, 1325 June 26, of land in Hooke (Dorset) to John de Barkingdon]

> [Lease, 1586 June 10, of the manor of White Waltham (Berks.) to Thomas Grove]

> [Quitclaim, 1290 June 27, of rights in the manor of Washfield (Devon) to Henry le Abbe]

> [Marriage settlement, 1665 April 20, between Alice Meredith Croft and John Maende]

For unbound collections of single legal documents and archival records, supply a title consisting of a word or brief phrase characterizing the type of documents making up the collection and as many of the title elements given above for a single legal document or archival record as is consistent with the collection as a whole, but giving at least the extreme range of dates covered by the material. When appropriate, also include as part of the supplied title bulk dates for the material. Enclose bulk dates in parentheses with the designation *bulk* and following the inclusive dates.

> [Writs, 1356–1642]

> [Manor court rolls, 1282–1419 (bulk 1350–1419)]

For bound collections of compiled legal documents and archival records, supply a title consisting of a word or phrase characterizing either the type of collection itself or the type of documents making up the collection and as many of the title elements given above for a single legal document or archival record as is consistent with the collection as a whole, but giving at least the extreme range of dates covered by the material. When appropriate, also include as part of the supplied title bulk dates for the material. Enclose bulk dates in parentheses with the designation *bulk* and following the inclusive dates.

> [Cartulary, 955–1316]

> [Register of writs, 1295–1415]

> [Mercantile records, 1476–1502 (bulk 1495–1502)]

1C. GENERAL MATERIAL DESIGNATION *(OPTIONAL ADDITION)*

Supply the appropriate general material designation immediately following the title proper as instructed in *AACR2R* 1.1C.

1D. PARALLEL TITLES

1D1

If a parallel title is a grammatically integral part of the title information, transcribe it as part of the title proper (see 1B1).

1D2

If a parallel title is not a grammatically integral part of the title information, transcribe it in a note for variations of title.

1E. OTHER TITLE INFORMATION

1E1

Transcribe all other title information following the chief title. Do not abridge other title information.

> Regula Beati Francisci : confirmata a domino Pape Honorio

> Officium Beate Marie Virginis : secundum consuetudinem Romane curie

> The inventarye of all the goodes and chattells of John Edolf, late of New Romnye, gent., deceased : taken and priced the xx. daie of Septemb[e]r 1576 in the xviii. yere of the raigne of o[u]r soveraign ladye Quene Elisabeth

> (**Source of information, at head of page:** *The inuentarye of all the goodes and Chattells of iohn Edolf late of New Romnye gent. deceased taken and priced the xx. daie of Septembr 1576 in the xviij. yere of the raigne of o͏ʳ soueraign Ladye Quene Elisabeth.*)
>
> [Dawson and Kennedy-Skipton, *Elizabethan Handwriting*, no. 15]

> L'ordre [et] police gardez en l'institution de l'Appotiquairerye, College [et] Chapelle de la Charité Chrestienne : pour les pauvres honteux, prestres, escoliers, gentilzhommes, marchans [et] artisans de la ville [et] faulxbourgs de Paris, detenus en extremite de maladie / de l'invention de Nicolas Houël, Parisien

> (**Source of information, title page:** *L'ORDRE & Police gardez en l'institution de l'Appotiquairerye, College & Chapelle de la Charité Chrestienne, pour les pauures honteux, Prestres, Escoliers, Gentilzhommes, Marchans & Artisans de la ville & faulxbourgs de Paris, Detenus en extremite de maladie. De l'inuention de Nicolas Houël Parisien.*)
>
> [BnF, *Manuscrits*, 103–4]

1E2

If a title proper needs explanation, supply a brief addition in the language of the cataloging agency enclosed in square brackets as other title information.

Propheta magnus surrexit : [sermon on Luke XIV,10]

[Book of hours : use of Paris]

1F. STATEMENTS OF RESPONSIBILITY

1F1

Transcribe an explicit statement of responsibility appearing in conjunction with or as a grammatically integral part of title information as it appears in the source. If an explicit statement of responsibility is not present, neither construct or extract one from the content of an item, nor supply one. Do not abridge the statement of responsibility. Record the names of scribes, notaries, and witnesses, etc. in a note.

Legenda aurea / de Iocabo de Voragine

Marci Catonis vita / per Leonardum Arretinum e Plutarcho in Latinum traducta

Le livre des proprietes des choses / translate de Latin en Francois l'an mil trois cens sexante et douze par le commandement du Roy Charles le quint de son nom regnant en France noblement et puissaument en ce temps

Cassiodori Senatoris De institutionibus divinarum litterarum

Additiones domini Prioris Petri super Regula Sancti Salvatoris

Liber … hystorie gentis Anglorum

(**Sources of information, opening rubric**: *Incipit prologus venerabilis bede presbiteri.* ; **closing rubric**: *Explicit liber .v. hystorie gentis anglorum.* **NB** *Author identified as the Venerable Bede in opening rubric, but not in conjunction with the title proper.*)

[Shailor, *Beinecke Library*, II:152]

1F2

If the only statement of responsibility present is one that has been added at a later date (that is, absent from the chief source of information, being in a script later than that of the main body of text), transcribe this statement in square brackets and provide a note indicating its nature and source.

Rationale divinorum officiorum / [Wilelmus Durhant]

(**Sources of information, opening rubric [chapter list]:** *Hic incipiunt rubrice libris Rationalis divinorum officiorum qui s. liber dividitur in 8 partes ...;* **opening rubric [prologue]** *Racionale divinorum officiorum incipit Rubrica. ;* **closing rubric:** *Explicit rationale divinorum officiorum. ; added on fol. iii verso by a 15th-cent. English hand: "Wilelmus Durhant [corrected to "Durandus" by a 17th-cent. hand] erat nomen compilatoris huius libri ut dictum est.")*

[Dutschke, *Huntington Library*, II:655–56]

1F3

If a statement of responsibility precedes the title proper in the chief source of information and it is not a grammatically integral part of the title proper, transpose it to its required position following the title proper and other title information. Do not use the mark of omission. Indicate the original position of the statement of responsibility in a note.

1F4

If there is more than one statement of responsibility appearing in conjunction with the title and statement of responsibility, transcribe them in the order in which they appear. If a subsequent statement of responsibility appears elsewhere in an item, transcribe it in a note.

Della nobilita civile / de M. Girolamo Osorio ; Portoghese tradotta in lingua Italiana de Bernado Trivigiano

1F5

Include all titles of nobility, address, honor, distinction, reverence, office, membership in societies, and other qualifications or descriptions that accompany names in a statement of responsibility.

Liber dyalogorum Beati Gregorii Pape Doctoris

Anicii Manlii Severini Boetii viri illustris et consularis ordinarii patricii Liber de consolatione philosophie

De regimine principum / editus a Fratre Egidio Romano Ordinis Fratrum Heremitarum Sancti Augustini

La controversie de noblesse plaidoyee entre Publius Cornelius Scipion dune part et Gaius Flaminius de aultre part / laquelle a este faicte et composee par un notable docteur en loix et grant orateur nomme Surse de Pistoye'

1F6

If an explicit statement of responsibility for an item is incorrect or obsolete, and is not simply a variant form of the author's name, give the correct or current attribution enclosed in square brackets. Transcribe in a note the incorrect or obsolete attribution.

2. EDITION / VERSION AREA

CONTENTS

2A. PRELIMINARY RULE

2A1. Scope

Use this area only to record explicit statements of edition or version appearing in an item. Do not use this area to describe the recension of a text within its manuscript tradition—place such information in a note, if desired. If an item was clearly intended as a draft, or it if carries markings indicating that it was a stationer's exemplar (marked "pecia" or "p" in the margin), record this information in a note for origin (see 7B14). It will be rare that any manuscript will have a true edition or version statement. Use of this area will be very limited.

2A2. Punctuation

For instructions on the use of spaces before and after prescribed punctuation, see 0C.

Precede this area by a full stop, space, dash, space.

Precede the first statement of responsibility following an edition statement by a diagonal slash.

Precede each subsequent statement of responsibility by a semicolon.

2A3. Sources of information

Take information recorded in this area from the chief source of information. Record in a note the location within an item where this information was obtained. Enclose in square brackets all information taken from alternate sources of information.

2B. Edition / version statement

2B1

If an explicit statement of edition or version appears as a grammatically integral part of a title proper, transcribe it as part of the title proper.

2B2

If an explicit statement of edition or version appears anywhere else in an item not in conjunction with the title proper, transcribe this statement in the edition / version area. If this statement appears in a hand later than that of the text, either within the item or on the binding or dorse, transcribe this statement and enclose it in square brackets. Whenever a statement of edition or version is transcribed separately from the title proper provide a note detailing the source.

> versio ultima

2C. Statements of responsibility relating to the edition or version

Transcribe an explicit statement of responsibility relating to an edition or version of a work according to the rules given above in 2B1 and 2B2.

3. MATERIAL SPECIFIC DETAILS AREA

3A

This area is not used for manuscripts.

4. PLACE AND DATE OF PRODUCTION AREA

CONTENTS

4A. PRELIMINARY RULES

4A1. Scope

Use this area for literary manuscripts only. Do not record the place and date of production for letters, legal documents, or archival records here, as this information is already given as an element of the supplied title for such items (see 1B2).

4A2. Punctuation

For instructions on the use of spaces before and after prescribed punctuation, see 0C.

Precede this area by a full stop, space, dash, space.

Precede the date of production by a comma.

4A3. Sources of information

Take information recorded in this area from the chief source of information. Seek information first from a colophon or other explicit statement of place or date of production. Lacking such an explicit statement, derive information from any available localizable or datable textual or physical evidence (*e.g.*, content, script, decoration, etc.). Record in a note the location within an item from which this information is obtained and the features on which it is based. If information is obtained from an alternate source of information, such as a reference work, published article, or scholarly communication, etc., record this source in a note. Enclose all information taken from alternate sources of information in square brackets.

If an item is an exact microform, photographic, or electronic reproduction, record information in this area appropriate to the *original*. Give details relating to the *reproduction* in a note.

4B. General rules

4B1
Record information in this area relating to the place and date of production of an item.[18]

4B2
Supply place and date of production information in this area as accurately as available evidence will permit and enclose this information in square brackets.

Transcribe information in this area only as permitted in the specific rules below, in which case *do not* enclose this information in square brackets. If an item contains an explicit statement of place or date of production, such as a colophon, transcribe this statement in a note for origin (see 7B14).

4B3
If an item purports to have been produced in or at an incorrect or fictitious place and/or date, supply only a corrected place and/or date of production in this area. Transcribe an incorrect or fictitious attribution in a note for origin (see 7B14).

4C. Place of production

4C1
Supply a place of production for an item, as accurately as available evidence will allow, giving the place, region, or country of production in its modern form enclosed in square brackets. Do not give cardinal locations (*e.g.*, southern Germany) in this area. Provide details of localization in a note for origin (see 7B14).

> [Spain]

---

18. *AMREMM* departs significantly from *AACR2R*, *APPM*, and *DCRB* in the treatment of this area. *AACR2R* treats all manuscripts as "unpublished items" (1.4C8, 1.4D9, 1.4F9) and does not record place or agency of production information for manuscripts in this area, although it does record date of production information (1.4F9, 4.4B1). *APPM* does not record any of this information in this area (1.4). *AACR2R* and *DCRB* emphasize transcription of information in this area to greater or lesser degree (*AACR2R* 1.4B4, 1.4C1, 1.4D2, 1.4D3, 1.4F1, 1.4F2, 2.16B, 2.16D, 2.16F, 4.4B1; *DCRB* 4A3). *AMREMM* recognizes the value of place and date of production information to researchers of pre-modern manuscripts and accommodates this information in this area to facilitate ready identification and retrieval. However, manuscripts rarely contain explicit place, agency, or date of production information and the physical and textual evidence for their dating, localization, and identification of agency of production is the subject of scholarly research and interpretation. Even when explicit information such as a colophon is present, this information must still be mediated by the bibliographical specialist for precision and is better transcribed in full elsewhere in a note (see 7B14). Thus, *AMREMM* provides place and date of production information in this area when it is available, though not agency of production information, and favors supplied information in a modernized form rather than transcribed information in its original form.

[France]

[Brittany]

[Osnabrück]

(**Source of information, colophon**: *Scriptum … in conventu Osnaburgensi per me fr. Ioannem Schyphower …*)

[*Colophons*, III:484, #11,355]

If the original form of the place of production as it appears in the item corresponds to the modern form of the name in the language of the cataloging agency, transcribe the original form and omit the use of square brackets. If the place of production has no modern form or no longer exists, transcribe the original form from the source in the nominative or oblique case and omit the use of square brackets. Transcribe any explicit place of production information appearing in the item in a note for origin (see 7B14).

Paris

(**Source of information, colophon**: *Richart de Monbaston, libraire, a fait escrire ceste legende des sains en françois lan de grace 1348 demeurant a Paris en la rue neufve nostre Dame*)

[*Colophons*, V:231, #16,578]

4C2

If the attribution of a place of production is conjectural or uncertain, follow the place of production with a question mark.

[England?]

[Siena?]

If no place or probable place of production can be determined, omit the place of production element for this area.

4C3

If an item is a composite codex manuscript whose constituent parts were produced in different localities, record for the place of production of the host item the widest geographical area common to all parts. If the constituent parts do not share at least a common country of production, do not record a place of production in this area, but instead list the separate places of production in a note. If the constituent parts are separately analyzed, supply the place of production in this area for each as appropriate. Give the place at which a composite codex manuscript was created, if this can be ascertained, in a note for origin (see 7B14).

4D. Date of production

4D1

Supply a date of production for an item as accurately as available evidence will allow, giving the date expressed in Arabic numerals as a year or range of years. Convert all dating systems to the New Style of the Gregorian calendar (see 1B2.1). If the original form of the date as it appears in the item already corresponds to the Arabic numeral, New Style Gregorian form, transcribe the original form and omit the use of square brackets. Transcribe any explicit date of production information appearing in the item in a note for origin (see 7B14).

[1399]

(***Source of information, colophon***: *Iste liber est Sancti Victoris iuxta Parisius, quem fecit scribere frater Iohannes de Villaribus anno Domini millesimo CCC^{mo} nonagesimo nono.*)

[Samaran and Marichal, *Manuscrits en écriture latine*, I:247]

[1271]

(***Source of information, colophon***: *Escrit fu en l'an de l'incarnation N[ost]re Seignor Jhesu Crist M et II^c et LXX, o meis de jenvier.* **N.B.** *year beginning March 1*)

[Samaran and Marichal, *Manuscrits en écriture latine*, I:35]

[1455]

(***Source of information, colophon***: *Iste liber fuit finitus per manum Iohannis Masseri … anno Domini 1454 in ianuario …* **N.B.** *year beginning March 1*)

[Samaran and Marichal, *Manuscrits en écriture latine*, I:363]

1474

(***Source of information, colophon***: *… finita per guilhelmum de Elden Anno domini 1474. 28 die Mensis Novembris.*)

[Lieftinck and Gumbert, *Manuscrits dans les Pays-Bas*, II:149]

4D2

If no exact date can be established for an item, supply an approximate, probable, or known date or range of dates based upon localizable or datable textual or physical evidence (*e.g.*, content, script, decoration, etc.). In assigning a date, particularly on the basis of physical evidence, the difference between an approximate or probable date and a known date depends upon the judgment of the cataloger. Assign dates following the paradigm set out below.

[1215?]	*probable exact date*
[ca. 1350]	*approximate date*

[ca. 1350?]	*probable approximate date*
[1415?–1460]	*date range between a probable terminus ante quem and a known terminus post quem*
[112–]	*known decade*
[112–?]	*probable decade*
[11––]	*known century*
[11––?]	*probable century*
[between 11–– and 12––]	*date range within known centuries*
[between 11––? and 12––?]	*date range within probable centuries*
[between 1100 and 1125]*	*known date range within the beginning/first-quarter of the twelfth century*
[between 1125 and 1150]	*known date range within the second-quarter of the twelfth century*
[between 1100 and 1150]*	*known date range within the first-half of the twelfth century*
[between 1125 and 1175]	*known date range within the middle of the twelfth century*
[between 1150 and 1199]*	*known date range within the second-half of the twelfth century*
[between 1150 and 1175]	*known date range within the third-quarter of the twelfth century*
[between 1175 and 1199]*	*known date range within the end/fourth-quarter of the twelfth century*
[between 1175 and 1225]	*known date range within the end/fourth-quarter of the twelfth century and the beginning/first-quarter of the thirteenth century*

*Centuries are both recorded in this area and customarily coded in the fixed fields as running from 00 to 99, although a century properly runs from 01 to 00. This practice results in the truncation by one year of date ranges that extend to the end of a century, but it ensures agreement of date expressions between this area and the fixed fields so that items will file within their appropriate centuries.

4D3

If an item is a composite codex manuscript whose constituent parts were produced at different times, record for the date of production of the host item the widest range of dates of production for all parts. If the constituent parts are separately analyzed, record the date of production in this area for each as appropriate. Give the date at which a composite codex manuscript was created, if this can be ascertained, in a note for origin (see 7B14).

5. PHYSICAL DESCRIPTION AREA

Contents

5A. PRELIMINARY RULE

5A1. Punctuation
For instruction on the use of spaces before and after prescribed punctuation, see section 0C.

Precede this area with a full stop, space, dash, space or start a new paragraph.

Precede details of illustration or illumination by a colon.

Precede dimensions by a semicolon.

Precede each statement of accompanying materials by a plus sign.

Enclose physical details of accompanying materials in parentheses.

5A2. Sources of information
Take information recorded in this area from the item itself.

5A3
If an item is an exact microform, photographic, or electronic reproduction, record information in this area appropriate to the *original*. Give details relating to the *reproduction* in a note.

5B. Extent

Single volumes or items

5B1

Record the total extent of an item according to the terminology suggested by the physical format of the manuscript. Generally, describe a manuscript in terms of leaves, regardless of whether the manuscript is foliated or paginated, or whether these leaves are written on both sides or only one, or whether these leaves only carry illustration or illumination, or are blank. Describe a manuscript consisting of only a single leaf as a leaf. Describe a manuscript consisting of only two conjugate leaves as a bifolium. Describe all other arrangements in terms of leaves, regardless of conjugacy. Thus, do not describe a manuscript consisting of four leaves made up of two conjugate pairs as two bifolia; rather, describe it as four leaves. Describe individual, unbound single- or multiple-sheet legal documents in terms of sheets. Describe items in the form of a roll in terms of a roll. For parchment and paper rolls, describe and give the number of their constituent parts (attached head to tail or head to head) in terms of membranes for parchment rolls or in terms of sheets for paper rolls, enclosing this information in parentheses immediately following the specific material designation for the roll itself. Describe manuscript fragments in terms of items.

5B2

Give the total number of leaves, sheets, or membranes making up an item, followed by the appropriate specific material designation. Count all leaves or sheets before recording the extent. Do not rely upon any numeration present in a manuscript, whether original or added later; instead, supply this information as part of the note for the statement of collation (see 7B7.1b). Include in the total extent original raised flyleaves, original flyleaves used as pastedown or free-end endpapers, and blanks. Do not include in the total extent canceled leaves, or modern flyleaves and endpapers. Do not enclose the total extent in square brackets.

> 1 leaf
>
> 1 bifolium
>
> 125 leaves
>
> 2 sheets
>
> 1 roll (5 sheets)
>
> 1 roll (8 membranes)
>
> 1 item

Do not record any sequences of foliation, pagination, or other numeration in this area. Record such information, instead, in the appropriate part of a note for the statement of collation (see 7B7.1b).

AACR2R 4.5B1 makes provision for recording certain layout features, such as number of columns and lines per page, within the statement of extent. Record this information, instead, in a note for layout (see 7B8).

5B3

When giving the extent for a component part of a larger item, record the range of leaves or pages occupied by the component part. Use the numeration employed in the manuscript itself that is recognized by the holding institution to be standard for purposes of citation (*i.e.*, do not use superceded sequences of numeration that may be present). The numeration of the range of leaves or pages given as the extent for a component part must correspond to the numeration given for the same work in the contents note of the host item.

> leaves 5r–30v

> leaves 1r–26v, 26r [bis]

> p. 10–15

Multiple volumes or items

5B4

If a manuscript exists in more than one volume or other specific material designation, give the total number of volumes or other specific material designation immediately followed in parentheses by the total number of leaves, sheets, or membranes in each.

> 2 v. (200, 150 leaves)

> 3 rolls (8, 5, 10 membranes)

5B5

For unbound collections of individual letters, legal documents, or archival records give the total number of such documents in terms of items. Do not describe them in terms of linear feet.

> 83 items

5C. Physical details

5C1. Support
Name the material that serves as the writing support for an item. If the material is parchment or vellum, use the term "parchment" as the more generic, regardless of the quality of the material.

> 20 leaves : parchment

15 leaves : paper

7 leaves : papyrus

1 sheet : parchment

1 roll (10 membranes) : parchment

1 roll (5 sheets) : paper

1 roll : papyrus

5C2. Illustrative matter

Describe any illustrations, illuminations, calendars, canon tables, genealogical tables, diagrams, etc. as *ill.* in all cases, unless there are maps present. If maps are present, give their total number. For purposes of recording information in this area, simple pen-flourished initials, line fillers, decorated catchwords, etc. are not considered as illustration or illumination. Describe these features in a note for decoration if desired. Provide details appropriate to the level of cataloging on illustration, illumination, maps, etc. in a note for decoration (see 7B10).

93 leaves : parchment, ill.

60 leaves : parchment, ill., 2 maps

5D. DIMENSIONS

5D1

Give the dimensions of a manuscript measuring first height and then width in millimeters, rounding to the nearest whole millimeter. Dimensions throughout a manuscript may vary, so measurements given should be approximate dimensions representative of the whole. Give dimensions first for the leaf, then (in parentheses) for the written space, followed by the dimension as bound when appropriate. When providing dimensions for the written space, take note of the layout of the page whether the first line of text is written above the first line of ruling or below the first line of ruling (and thus frame ruled).[19] For manuscripts that lack frame ruling and are written above the top line, measure written space from the headline or the top of minims in the first line of writing in the text to the baseline or the

---

19. Between the last decades of the twelfth century and the second quarter of the thirteenth, scribal practice shifted from writing above the first line of ruling to writing below the first line of ruling; that is, a shift from leaving the text block open at the top margin of the page to enclosing the text block within a frame of ruled lines. From about the middle of the thirteenth century, the normal practice of scribes was to write the first line of text below the first line of ruling, thereby enclosing the text block in a ruled frame. The practice of writing above the line made a prominent reappearance in the fifteenth century as a conscious attempt to imitate the layout of supposed ancient manuscripts. See N.R. Ker, "From 'Above Top Line' to 'Below Top Line': A Change in Scribal Practice," *Celtica* 5 (1960): 13–16, rpt. in *Books, Collectors and Libraries:*

bottom of minims in the last line of writing in the text. For manuscripts that are frame ruled and written below the first line of ruling, measure written space from the top bounding line of the frame ruling to the bottom bounding line of the frame ruling. Dimensions for width in all cases should be measured across columns and between outer vertical bounding lines or, where these do no exist or prove unsatisfactory, between the ends of a line of text. Where dimensions of the text block and the frame ruling differ significantly, measure the actual written space. Details on ruling patterns and their dimensions may be given in a note for layout (see 7B8).

Include within the dimensions of the written space any marginal gloss or commentary executed as part of the original text block, such as in the case of glossed biblical, legal, or philosophical texts.[20] Dimensions of the gloss or commentary may, in addition, be given separately as part of the note for layout if desired. Do not include within the dimensions of the written space marginal glosses, commentary, or other annotations in a script or hand later than the script or hand of the main body of text. If it cannot be determined whether the marginal gloss or commentary was executed as part of the original text, give dimensions for the main body of text only and provide dimensions of the gloss or commentary in the note for layout. Also include within the dimensions of the written space any illustration, illumination, or other decoration situated within the text.

> 60 leaves : parchment ; 254 x 171 (209 x 121) mm. bound to 259 x 176 mm.

Where leaf or other dimensions differ significantly throughout an item (e.g., from uneven trimming or damage), express dimensions as a range.

> 95 leaves : parchment ; 236–246 x 176 (190 x 132) mm. bound to 253 x 183 mm.

5D2

For texts written in irregular lines of verse across the page, give as dimensions for the written space only the vertical measurement extending either from the headline or top of minims in the first line of writing in the text to the baseline or the bottom of minims in the last line of writing in the text, or if the manuscript is frame ruled from the top bounding line of the frame ruling to the bottom bounding line of the frame ruling.

> 10 leaves : parchment ; 200 x 150 (160) mm. bound to 210 x 160 mm.

Studies in the Medieval Heritage, ed. Andrew G. Watson (London: Hambledon Press, 1985), 71–74; Ker, *MMBL*, I:viii–ix; Albert Derolez, *Codicologie des manuscrits en écriture humanistique sur parchemin*, 2 vols., Bibliologia: Elementa ad librorum studia pertinentia, 5–6 (Turnhout: Brepols, 1984), I:82–85; Marco Palma, "Modifiche di alcuni aspetti materiali della produzione libraria latina nei secoli XII e XIII," *Scritura e civiltà* 12 (1988): 119–33. Cf. Jacques Lemaire, *Introduction à la codicologie*, Publications de l'Institut d'études médiévales: textes, études, congrès, 9 (Louvain-la-Neuve: Université catholique de Louvain, 1989), 163–64.

20. On the layout, ruling, and copying of glossed texts of the Bible see Christopher de Hamel, *Glossed Books of the Bible and the Origins of the Paris Booktrade* (Woodbridge, Suffolk: D.S. Brewer, 1984), 14–37.

5D3

For individual letters, legal documents, and archival records, give dimensions for the leaf or sheet only. Do not record dimensions of the written space for these materials. If these materials were originally or subsequently folded, give dimensions as laid open.

> 1 sheet : parchment ; 230 x 380 mm.

5D4

For items in the form of a roll, give the total length and width of the roll. Do not record dimensions of the written space for these materials.

> 1 roll (10 membranes) : parchment ; 3000 x 300 mm.

> 1 roll (4 sheets) : paper ; 1200 x 300 mm.

5E. ACCOMPANYING MATERIAL

5E1

Give details of accompanying materials. Briefly give the number and the name of accompanying materials at the end of the physical description. Detailed description may be provided in a note. Letters and legal documents, in particular, frequently bear seals. Record in this area only seals that are physically present (either intact or fragmentary), not those that were once attached but have been subsequently removed or lost. Record detailed descriptions of seals and any evidence for seals no longer present in a note for accompanying materials (see 7B13).

> 1 sheet : parchment ; 160 x 300 mm. + 2 seals

6. SERIES AREA

6A

This area is not used for manuscripts.

7. NOTE AREA

Contents

       7B18. Bynames
       7B19. Current shelfmark
       7B20. Reference to published descriptions or citations
       7B21. Reference to published editions, facsimiles, or treatments
       7B22. Additional physical form
       7B23. Form of reproduction
       7B24. Restrictions on access
       7B25. Terms governing use and reproduction
       7B26. Location of originals / reproductions
       7B27. Cataloging history

7A. Preliminary rule

7A1. Punctuation

Precede each note by a full stop, space, dash, space or start a new paragraph.

Separate introductory wording from the main content of a note by a colon followed, but not preceded by, a space.

7A2. Sources of information

Take data recorded in notes from any suitable source. Square brackets are required for interpolations within quoted material and as set out in 7A3.

7A3. Transcription and editorial practice in notes

A cataloging agency may employ in the note area any method of transcribing source text deemed appropriate, so long as that method is a clear and consistent one. It is recommended that the method defined for use in the title and statement of responsibility area (see 0F1–0F8) also be applied as a minimum standard for transcription in the notes, although abbreviations may be expanded silently in order to provide a more easily readable text. If a more detailed transcription is desired to record certain characteristics of the text, such as original punctuation, or additions, suppressions, or substitutions to the text, a cataloging agency may choose to employ a semi-diplomatic method of transcription.[21]

Enclose transcribed text in the notes in quotation marks. The method for representing the extent of a work present in a given manuscript is generally to transcribe portions of the text of that work in the following order:

- Opening rubric
- Incipit
- Explicit
- Closing rubric

---

21. See, *e.g.*, François Masai, "Principes et conventions de l'édition diplomatique," *Scriptorium* 4 (1950): 177–93; Anthony G. Petti, *English Literary Hands from Chaucer to Dryden* (Cambridge, Mass.: Harvard University Press, 1977), 34–35.

Precede transcribed rubrics with the designation "[rubr.]" and precede the incipit of the following text with the designation "[text]" (printed manuscript catalogs customarily distinguish rubrics from text through the use of alternating italic and roman type faces). Transcribe rubrics in full. Transcribe as much of an incipit as will distinguish a particular text or version of a work and as much of an explicit as will indicate the extent and conclusion of that text. Use the mark of omission to indicate the continuity of any untranscribed text between opening rubric, incipit, explicit, and closing rubric. Where the continuity of the text of a work broken, transcribe the text immediately preceding and following the discontinuity. Thus,

"[rubr.] *opening rubric.* [text] *incipit … explicit.* [rubr.] *closing rubric.*"

See 7B5.2 for examples.

7A4. Notes required in the catalog record

The following notes required in the catalog record define only a minimum set of notes for each level of description. Notes may be selectively augmented, abbreviated, or added according to local cataloging policies and requirements. For instance, an institution choosing to create summary descriptions for its holdings may wish to emphasize the decorative elements of these materials and so provide extensive notes on decoration equivalent to those normally given in a detailed description. In all cases, information is supplied on the basis of its applicability and availability.[22]

Distinctions between summary and detailed description are not absolute. Both levels of description contain virtually the same set of notes (detailed description, for instance, adds notes on Statement of collation and Accompanying materials), but the meaningful difference lies in the degree of detail that

7A4.1. Notes required in a summary description

A summary description requires at least all the notes set out below to be included in the catalog record, if applicable and available:

7B1. Format, nature, and scope
7B2. Language
7B3. Source of title proper and statement of responsibility

7A4.2. Notes required in a detailed description

A detailed description requires at least all the notes set out below to be included in the catalog record, if applicable and available:

7B1. Format, nature, and scope
7B2. Language
7B3. Source of title proper and statement of responsibility
7B4. Variations of title and statement of responsibility

---

22. Availability of information can be highly variable. It depends in each case upon the expertise either possessed by the individual cataloger or provided by a bibliographical specialist or by an already existing description. For instance, an inability to identify precisely a grade of script or decorative feature renders that information unavailable.

7B5.	Contents	7B5.	Contents	*(full note)*
		7B7.	Statement of collation	
7B8.	Layout *(brief note indicating number of columns and lines of text)*	7B8.	Layout *(full note)*	
7B9.	Script *(brief note indicating general type of script)*	7B9.	Script *(full note)*	
7B10.	Decoration *(brief note indicating presence of illumination or other significant decoration)*	7B10.	Decoration *(full note)*	
7B11.	Music *(brief note indicating presence of music)*	7B11.	Music *(full note)*	
7B12.	Binding *(brief note identifying binding as contemporary or modern)*	7B12.	Binding *(full note)*	
7B13.	Accompanying materials *(brief note)*	7B13.	Accompanying materials *(full note)*	
7B14.	Origin *(brief note indicating immediately identifiable place, date, and agency of production, i.e. colophon)*	7B14.	Origin *(full note)*	
		7B15.	Provenance	
		7B16.	Immediate source of acquisition	
7B17.	Former and related shelfmarks	7B17.	Former and related shelfmarks	
7B18.	Bynames	7B18.	Bynames	
7B19.	Current shelfmark	7B19.	Current shelfmark	
7B20.	Reference to published descriptions or citations	7B20.	Reference to published descriptions or citations	
7B21.	Reference to published editions, facsimiles, or treatments	7B21.	Reference to published editions, facsimiles, or treatments	
7B23.	Form of reproduction	7B23.	Form of reproduction	
7B27.	Cataloging history	7B27.	Cataloging history	

each conveys and the amount of expertise and judgment required to provide that additional information. Outlines for summary and detailed descriptions are supplied here as guides in determining the amount of work required for each record. Summary description may be characterized as containing information that is immediately observable or identifiable and detailed description as containing fuller information resulting from further examination and research.

7B. Notes
Generally, make notes as set out below and in the order given. At any point, a general note may be introduced to provide supplemental or related information to any of the specific notes below. Group associated notes together. A general note may also be introduced at any appropriate point in the description to record information not addressed by any of the specific notes below.

7B1. Format, nature, and scope
Make notes on the format, nature, and scope of a manuscript or manuscript collection.

7B1.1

Give brief information on the physical format of an item or items. Use one of the following designations as appropriate:

Ms. or Mss.	*Apply generally to all manuscript items not addressed more specifically below.*

Whenever possible, apply one of the following specific designations:

Ms. fragment(s)	*Apply to an item or items consisting of a portion excised or remaining from a MS. LEAF or from the sheet or leaf of a letter, legal document, or archival record, etc. (e.g., a cutting of an illuminated initial, a heavily damaged leaf). If these fragments are from disparate leaves or sheets, indicate this fact further in the note for nature and scope.*
Ms. leaf or leaves	*Apply to an item or items consisting of one or more individual leaves or sheets or unsewn bifolia remaining or excised from a MS. CODEX. If these leaves are from disparate manuscript codices, indicate this fact at a later point in the note for nature and scope.*
Ms. gathering(s)	*Apply to an item or items consisting of two or more sewn bifolia or combination of sewn bifolia and disjunct leaves remaining or excised from a MS. CODEX.*
Ms. component part	*Apply only to an item (i.e., work) given separate analysis (see Appendix B) that is part of a MS. CODEX for which a host-item catalog record also exists.*
Ms. codex	*Apply to an item consisting of one or more sewn gatherings bound together constituting a book. Designate a MS. CODEX that has been dismembered or damaged to such an extent that it no longer presents a single coherent work as MS. FRAGMENTS(S), MS. LEAF or LEAVES, or MS. GATHERINGS(S). For instance, if all that remains of a MS. CODEX is a single quire of eight leaves containing chapter 2 of a larger work, designate this item as MS. GATHERING. However, if this quire contains the whole of the work, designate the item as MS. CODEX.*
Ms. composite codex	*Apply to a MS. CODEX composed of two or more physical parts of varying date of production and origin that have been subsequently bound together. Do not apply this designation to a MS. CODEX simply possessing fragments reused from another manuscript as flyleaves or binding material, or to a MS. CODEX containing multiple works of homogenous date of production and origin.*

Ms. document(s)	*Apply to an item or items constituting a letter, legal document, or archival record, regardless of physical format.*
Ms. roll(s)	*Apply to an item or items consisting of two or more paper sheets or parchment membranes joined together, or of a single long sheet or membrane, rolled to form a cylinder.*

7B1.2

Give a brief summary or abstract of the nature and scope of the contents of an item, if this information is not more appropriately treated elsewhere in the description. Give notice particularly of significant versions of a text or textual defects. Note also any physical defects in an item that also affect the text. If an item contains important or extensive glossing, commentary, or other annotation, make note of its presence. Also record whether an item possesses any special physical characteristics, such as whether it is a holograph, palimpsest, opisthograph, or chirograph or indenture. If the catalog record is intended to provide only an abstract in lieu of fuller information available elsewhere, such as an already published description (see 0B1.1, 7B20), provide a note indicating the nature and location of this fuller description.

> Bible arranged in usual order with common set of prologues (see Ker, *Medieval Manuscripts in British Libraries*, I: 96–97)

> Text of the Psalms with the Ordinary Gloss

> Text heavily annotated by a 16th-cent. hand

> Collection of 132 documents (1580–1710) pertaining to property holdings of the Hale family in Hertfordshire, Cambridgeshire, Bedfordshire, Berkshire, and London. The manors of King's Walden (Herts.), White Waltham (Berks.), and Edworth (Beds.) are particularly well documented

> See printed catalog for full description

7B2. Language

Identify the language or languages employed in an item and make concise notes on their use. For composite manuscript codices, briefly note the various languages employed throughout and provide more detailed notes in the records for individually analyzed works if desired.

> Latin

> Old French

> Latin, with interlinear glosses in Old English

> Latin and Old French

7B3. Source of title proper and statement of responsibility

Indicate the source of the title proper and statement of responsibility and the exact location within an item where the information is found, using the numeration employed in the manuscript itself that is recognized by the holding institution to be standard for purposes of citation. If the title proper and statement of responsibility is in a script or hand later than the main body of text of the manuscript, indicate an approximate date when it may have been added.

Title from rubric (fol. 2v)

Title from colophon (fol. 80r)

Title from table of contents (fol. 1r)

Title from spine, 17th cent.

Title added at head of text, 15th cent. (fol. 1r)

Title and statement of responsibility from printed catalog

Title supplied by cataloger

7B4. Variations of title and statement of responsibility

Make notes on significant variations of the title and statement of responsibility that are not already transcribed elsewhere. Transcribe these variations and indicate their location within an item. Also, transcribe parallel titles and other title information if they are considered to be important.

Running title (passim): Consulta Basilii

Title in prologue (fol. 1r): Regula Beati Basilii episcopi

Title in explicit (fol. 93v): Consulta Basilii que dicuntur regula eiusdem

7B5. Contents

7B5.1. General rules

7B5.1.1

The contents note functions in two capacities depending upon the level of description employed in the catalog record (see 0D) and the nature of the item itself. The format and the amount and complexity of information the contents note conveys are conditioned by a variety of factors: whether the manuscript contains a single work or a standard or compiled work or multiple works, the level of description in the catalog record, and the information available from the source. In the case of an item containing a single work, the contents note indicates the particular text or version of that work and the extent to which the text of that work is complete in the manuscript. In the case of an item containing a standard or compiled work or an item containing multiple works, it indicates the component works or items contained within the manuscript. Follow the instructions below for constructing the contents note. The particular examples given should be taken only as guides, not as prescriptive patterns, for formatting the contents note. The cataloger is free to improvise if none of the provisions given here satisfies the needs of the item being cataloged.

To determine the appropriate capacity and complexity of the contents note, follow the guide below according to the level of description employed and the nature of the contents of the item:

Summary description—

a) Single work
Do not provide a contents note

b) Standard or compiled work
Provide a contents note only for a compiled work according to 7B5.3

c) Multiple works
Provide a contents note according to 7B5.4

Detailed description—

a) Single work
Provide a contents note according to 7B5.2

b) Standard or compiled work
Provide a contents note according to 7B5.3

c) Multiple works
Provide a contents note for the host item according to 7B5.4, and a contents note for each separately analyzed work according to 7B5.2

7B5.1.2

Generally, list the contents of an item in full, including blank pages. Contents descriptions should present the fullest amount of information possible in a clear, accurate, and economical fashion. However, materials that are ancillary or of marginal significance may be summarized. The structure of the contents note should normally reflect the structure and order of elements as they appear in the manuscript. Assign Arabic numbers to each work or item contained in the manuscript according to the cataloger's division of its elements, beginning each entry as a separate paragraph. Precede each work or item contained in the manuscript with its folio or page reference (either inclusive or beginning folio or page). Provide references and commentary on the state of the text of the work or item as needed.

If information is not available to furnish a contents note according to any of the following rules, provide whatever information that is available in as clear and accurate a manner as possible.

7B5.2. Single work

Transcribe, in the order in which they appear, the opening rubric, incipit, explicit, and closing rubric for the text of a work. See 7A3 for methods of transcription.

> fol. 1r–4r:"[rubr.] Incipit regula sancti Augustini episcopi. [text] Ante omnia fratres karissimi diligatur Deus, deinde proximus … orans ut sibi debitum dimittatur et in temptationem non inducatur. [rubr.] Explicit regula sancti Augustini."

When a text is preceded by preliminary matter (*e.g.*, tables of contents, translator's prefaces, prologues, etc.) record at least the opening rubrics and incipits for these preliminaries. When a text is organized into books, parts, or other major divisions, record the opening rubrics, incipits, and explicits (and optionally the closing rubrics) for these divisions if considered necessary or desirable for clarity. If signaling the presence of these major divisions is not considered necessary or desirable, give only the opening rubric, incipit, explicit, and closing rubric of the entire text as shown above. Where confusion may arise in the designation of what is preliminary matter, major division, and main text, indicate in square brackets the part of the text being cited if this is not already made clear by the rubric or incipit itself.

> ### Contents note indicating translator's prologue, major divisions, and main text of a work in multiple books:
> (PL = Patrologia latina)
>
> 1. fol. 1r–33v:"[rubr.] Incipit prologus beati Iheronimi presbyteri in primum librum de vitis et doctrinis sanctorum patrum. [text] Benedictus Deus qui vult omnes homines salvos fieri … ; [fol. 2r: rubr.] Incipit liber primus de vitis et doctrinis sanctorum patrum editus ab Iheronimo. De sancto Iohanne abbate capitulum primum. [text] Primum igitur tamquam verum fundamentum nostri operis … et tanta nobis ostendit mirabilia ipsi gloria in secula seculorum. Amen. [rubr.] Explicit primus vitaspatrum." [PL 21:387–462].
> 2. fol. 33v–62v:"[rubr.] Incipit prologus in librum secundum. [text] Vere mundum quis dubitet meritis stare sanctorum … ; [fol. 34r: rubr.] Incipit liber secundus de verbis et doctrinis sanctorum patrum. [text] Quidam sanctorum seniorum patrum interrogantibus se monachis de causa abstinere dixit … quia interiori homini nostro sanitas inde crescit. [rubr.] Explicit liber secundus." [PL 73:739–810] …
>
> [Dutschke and Rouse, *Claremont Libraries*, 6–7]

> ### Simplified contents note indicating only the opening rubric and incipit of the prologue, and the opening rubric, incipit, explicit, and closing rubric of the text of a work complete in five books (major divisions not indicated):
>
> 1. fol. 1r: blank.

2. fol. 1v–149v: "[rubr.] Incipit prologus venerabilis Bede presbiteri. [text] Gloriosissimo regi Ceolvulfo Beda famulus christi et prespiter. Hystoriam gentis anglorum ecclesiasticam quam … ; [fol. 4r: rubr.] Britania oceani insula. [text] Cui quondam Albion nomen erat … letentur insule multe et confiteantur memorie sanctitatis eius. [rubr.] Explicit liber .v. hystorie gentis Anglorum."

[Shailor, Beinecke Library, II:152]

7B5.3. Standard or compiled work

For certain standard works whose contents vary within a defined set of texts (e.g., the Bible or liturgical and devotional works), or for compiled works (e.g., collections of sermons, hymns, letters, laws and statutes, charters, writs, and other legal documents, etc.), the normal sequence of opening rubrics, incipits, explicits, and closing rubrics need not be given. Instead, a cataloger's summary or supplied title, citation to a standard reference bibliography, or simply the rubric as it appears in the manuscript—or a combination of all of these—may be used. It may, however, be desirable in certain instances to transcribe the opening rubrics, incipits, explicits, and closing rubrics for the sake of clarity and accuracy.

Bible:
(Two examples showing increasing levels of complexity and detail for the same work, though not for the same manuscript.)

fol. 1r–612v: Bible in usual order (see Ker, *Medieval Manuscripts in British Libraries* I:96–97), prologues cited precede text: General Prologue [Stegmüller 284]; Prologue to Pentateuch [Stegmüller 285], Genesis, Exodus, Leviticus, Numbers, Deuteronomy; Joshua [Stegmüller 311]; Judges; Ruth; 1 Kings [Stegmüller 323] …

[Shailor, Beinecke Library, II:298]

fol. 1r–344v, Old Testament. fol. 1r–3r: "[rubr.] Incipit epistola beati Ieronimi ad Paulinum presbiterum de omnibus divinis historiis libris." [Stegmüller 284]; fol. 3r: "[rubr.] Alius prologus." [Stegmüller 285]; fol. 3r–18r: Genesis; fol. 18v–31r: "[rubr.] Incipit liber Exodi." fol. 31r–39v: "[rubr.] Incipit liber Levitici." fol. 39v–51v: "[rubr.] Incipit liber Numeri." fol. 51v–62r: "[rubr.] Incipit liber Deuteronomii." fol. 62r+v: "[rubr.] Incipit prologus super librum Iosue." [Stegmüller 311]; fol. 62v–70r: "[rubr.] Incipit liber Iosue." fol. 70r–77v: "[rubr.] Hic incipit liber Iudicum." fol. 77v–78v: "[rubr.] Incipit liber Ruth." fol. 78v–79r: "[rubr.] Prologus." [in Reg.; Stegmüller 323]; fol. 79r–90r: "[rubr.] Incipit liber Regum primus." …

[Dutschke and Rouse, Claremont Libraries, 18]

Book of Hours

1. fol. 1r–12v: Calendar including the feasts of Herculanus (1 March), Zenobius (25 May, in red), Proculus (1 June), Laurentinus and Pergentinus (3 June), Alexander bishop (6 June), Romulus (6 July), Nabor and Felix (12 July), Anne (26 July), "Sancte

Marie ad nives" (5 August, in red), Transfiguration (6 August, in red), Donatus (7 August), Concordia (13 August), Potitus (6 September), Salvius (10 September), Reparata (8 October, in red), Cerbonius (10 October), "Fidriani" [sic, for Frediano; 18 November], Florentinus bishop (30 December).

2. fol. 13r–111v: "[rubr.] Incipit offitium beate Marie virginis secundum consuetudinem romane curie."

3. fol. 112r–176v: Office of the Dead. fol. 177r+v ruled but blank.

4. fol. 178r–214r: Long Hours of the Cross. fol. 214v–215v ruled but blank.

5. fol. 216r–221r: Short Hours of the Cross. fol. 221v ruled but blank.

6. fol. 222r–239r: Penitential psalms.

7. fol. 239r–252r: Litany, including Zenobius. fol. 252v ruled but blank.

[Dutschke and Rouse, *Claremont Libraries*, 5–6]

Collection of Laws and Statutes: Magna Carta and Statutes to 12 Edward II

(SR = Statutes of the Realm)

1. fol. 1r–6v: Sarum calendar in purple, red, and black, partly graded. Added obit of "Thomas Minstrecha miles," A.D. 1452, at 19 Nov.

2. fol. 7v–12v: Table of statutes and chapters.

3. fol. 13r: "[rubr.] Magna carta. [text] Edwardus dei gracia ... T. Edwardo filio nostro apud Westm' xi [sic] die Octobris anno regni nostri xxv. Dat' per manum nostram apud Westm' xxviii die Marcii anno regni nostri xxix [sic]." [SR I:116].

4. fol. 20r: "[rubr.] Incipit sentencia eiusdem carta." [SR I:6].

5. fol. 21r: "[rubr.] Incipit carta de foresta." Confirmation of 12 [sic] Oct. 1297 [SR I:120].

6. fol. 24v: "[rubr.] Incipiunt provisiones de Merton." [SR I:1].

7. fol. 28v: "[rubr.] Incipit Statutum de Marlebergh." [SR I:19].

8. fol. 39r: "[rubr.] Incipit Statutum Westm' primi." In French. [SR I:26].

9. fol. 58r: "[rubr.] Incipit Statutum Gloucestr'." In French. [SR I:45].

10. fol. 63r: "[rubr.] Incipiunt explanaciones eiusdem." [SR I:50] ...

[N.R. Ker, *MMBL*, I:68]

7B5.4. Multiple works

For a manuscript containing multiple works or items for which separate analysis may or may not be provided, briefly list the contents of the manuscript using uniform or cataloger-supplied titles and author information. Prefer uniform titles and authorized forms of authors' names, but if titles exist in the manuscript these may be used if desired. If separate analysis is given to these works, provide a contents note for each analytic record according to the procedure given in 7B5.2.

1. fol. 1r–93v: Regula / Saint Basil, Bishop of Caesarea.

2. fol. 94r–160v: De institutis coenobiorum et de octo principalium vitiorum remediis libri XII / John Cassian.

3. fol. 161r–211v: Regula / Saint Benedict, Abbot of Monte Cassino.

4. fol. 211v–259v: Liber de praecepto et dispensatione / Saint Bernard of Clairvaux.
5. fol. 259v–268v: Praeceptum / Saint Augustine, Bishop of Hippo.

7B6. Secundo folio

Transcribe the opening word or words from the second leaf of a manuscript that may have been part of an institutional collection during the Middle Ages. Do not normally record *secundo folio* references for manuscripts commonly found, or known to have been, in private ownership during the Middle Ages (such as books of hours), for manuscripts from a period later than the Middle Ages, or for manuscripts that have clearly lost their second leaf at some later time. Precede this note with the heading *Secundo folio:*.

The *secundo folio* citation can refer equally to both the physical manuscript and the work it contains. Thus, if the second leaf of a manuscript is occupied by notes, tables of contents, calendars, canon tables, or other preliminary matter, transcribe the opening words for that second leaf, as well as the opening words of the text from the second leaf of a work contained in a manuscript. If a composite manuscript codex brings together at a later date works that may once have existed separately, it may be desirable to provide *secundo folio* references for each of those individual works. If the second leaf is occupied by text and accompanying commentary, give the opening words for both the text and the commentary. If the first word on the second leaf is subject to word division, supply the missing information in square brackets from the preceding leaf.

Secundo folio: desiderium flagrans

Secundo folio [text]: tempus predicte
Secundo folio [commentary]: Cum accessissent

Secundo folio [calendar, fol. 3r]: KL Marcius
Secundo folio [text, fol. 9r]: [in exi]tu hii

Certain regional medieval traditions of cataloging (e.g., Spain) systematically recorded the opening words of leaves other than those appearing on the second. If the provenance of an item places it within this context, transcribe this information under the note for *secundo folio* and provide a note detailing the special circumstance.

7B7. Statement of collation

The statement of collation consists of three parts:

1. Support and physical arrangement
2. Register of quires
3. Quire signatures, leaf signatures, and catchwords

Separate each part of the statement of collation from the one following it by a space-semi-colon-space. Follow the steps below in constructing the statement of collation. Enclose any necessary qualifying information in parentheses at the appropriate point in the statement to which it refers. Precede this note with the heading *Collation:*.

7B7.1 Support and physical arrangement

a) Specify the material, or support, on which an item is written. If the support is mixed, place at the head of the formula the predominant material used for support and register any differences in material used at the appropriate point in the formula. Identify watermarks in paper as clearly as possible with concise citation to standard reference sources.

> Parchment
> Paper (Briquet, Couronne, 4736)

b) Record the extent of an item by giving first the number of flyleaves at the front, then the number of leaves making up the body, and last the number of flyleaves at the end of the manuscript. Use lower-case roman numerals to designate flyleaves and Arabic numerals to designate leaves in the main body of the manuscript. Indicate the material used for the flyleaves and record any other information pertaining to them in parentheses at the point at which they are registered. Unless further qualification is given, the number of leaves given for the body of the manuscript is assumed also to express the present numeration of the manuscript—if any exists—by folio, regardless of whether that numeration is original or added later. If the leaves are paginated, or if there is a disturbance in the foliation, indicate the correct sequence in parentheses. Older sequences of numeration may be noted if desired. Flyleaves are assumed to be unnumbered, unless stated otherwise, and also to be contemporary with the binding unless stated otherwise. Concise remarks on the state of flyleaves or pastedowns may be included in the collational formula.

> fol. ii + 20 + ii
>
> fol. iii + 292 (foliated 1–11, 11*, 12–291) + iv
>
> fol. ii + 100 (paginated 1-200) + ii
>
> fol. ii (paper) + 150 + ii (paper)
>
> fol. ii (medieval parchment) + 245 + ii (medieval parchment)
>
> fol. ii (i is pastedown) + 58 + ii (ii is pastedown)

7B7.2 Register of quires

Record the sequence and composition of the quires that make up a manuscript. Use a formula to express collation that is clear, consistent, and as widely understood as possible. Use current Anglo-American conventions for manuscript collation based upon the system described by N.R. Ker, *Catalogue of Manuscripts Containing Anglo-Saxon* (Oxford, 1957), xxii (reprinted in *MMBL*, III:vii).[23]

$1–11^8(+9)$

$1^8 \; 2^8(+1, \text{fol. } 9, \text{ before } 1)$

$1^8 \; 2–4^{12} \; 5^{12}(+7, 8; \text{fol. } 51–52) \; 6–15^{12}$

$1–4^8 \; 5^8(\pm 4) \; 6–10^6 \; 11^6(4+1) \; 12^{10}(-3.8)$

$1^6(1 \text{ is pastedown}) \; 2–6^8 \; 7^6(6 \text{ is pastedown})$

$1^6 \; 2–6^8 \; 7^8(-8, \text{following fol. } 53, \text{ with loss of text}) \; 8–14^8 \; 15^2(\text{conjugate pair})$

$1–6^8 \mid 7–18^8 \mid 19–20^8$

$\text{I–XIII}^8, \text{XIV}^{10}(-2, 6 \text{ blanks})$

7B7.3 Quire signatures, leaf signatures, and catchwords

Make notes on the presence of quire signatures, leaf signatures, and catchwords at the end of the statement of collation.[24] The usual placement for quire signatures is presumed to be on the verso of the last leaf of each gathering; specify "on recto" if these appear instead on the recto of the first leaf of the gathering. The usual placement for leaf signatures is presumed to be on the recto of the first leaves of each gathering. The usual placement for catchwords is presumed to be at the bottom of the verso of the last leaf of each gathering; specify orientation (e.g., horizontal, vertical, diagonal) and location on leaf if otherwise.

Quires signed i–viii

Quires signed on recto I–X

Quires signed a–m

---

23. See also M. R. James, *A Descriptive Catalogue of the Manuscripts in the Fitzwilliam Museum* (Cambridge: Cambridge University Press, 1895), xix–xxiii. For historical and bibliographic orientation see Frank Bischoff, "Methoden der Lagenbeschreibung," *Scriptorium* 46 (1992): 3–27.

24. On the variety of forms and locations of quire signatures, leaf signatures, and catchwords, see Lemaire, *Introduction à la codicologie*, 61–67; Derolez, *Codicologie*, I:40–64; J. Vezin, "Observations sur l'emploi des réclames dans les manuscrits latins," *Bibliothèque de l'École des chartes* 125 (1967): 5–33; Ker, *MMBL*, I:ix–x.

Leaves signed aiii–giii

Horizontal catchwords in inner margin

Horizontal catchwords to right of center

Vertical catchwords

Decorated catchwords, leaves signed on recto a–d5, e4, f–g5

Example:

Collation: Parchment, fol. ii (paper: Briquet Armoiries, 1656) + 66 + ii (paper: Briquet Armoiries, 1656) ; 1–10^6 11^8(–2, 6) ; quires signed i–xi

Collation: Parchment, fol. iii (modern paper) + ii (medieval parchment, ruled but blank) + 248 + ii (medieval parchment, ruled but blank) + iii (modern paper) ; 1^2 2^8(–1, fol. 1, with loss of text) 3–10^{10} 11^{10}(–4, fol. 92, without loss of text) 12–26^{10} 27^2 ; horizontal catchwords in red ink frames

7B8. Layout[25]

Describe the page layout of an item to whatever degree and level is deemed appropriate. At a minimum, give notice of the number of lines of text, the number of columns (if more than one) into which the text is divided, and whether the text is plain ruled or frame-ruled. More detailed notes on layout may take account of whether text is written above or below the top line of ruling (see 5D1), ruling patterns, prickings in the margins, layout of glosses, etc. Precede this note with the heading *Layout:*.

Layout: Written in 25 long lines; frame-ruled

Layout: Written in 2 columns of 35 lines, above line; ruled

Layout: Written in 2 columns of 30 lines; frame-ruled in ink with double inner and outer vertical bounding lines; prickings in outer margin

Layout: Written in 2 columns, below top line, 20 lines for text, 40 lines for commentary. Text ruled in lead on alternate lines in inner column; continuous commentary ruled in dry point in outer column

---

25. *AACR2R* 4.5B1 makes provision for recording certain layout features, such as number of columns and lines per page, within the statement of extent. Record this information, instead, in a note for layout (cf. 5B2).

7B9. Script

Identify the script in which an item is written to whatever degree and level is deemed appropriate. At a minimum, identify the type and grade of script (*q.v.*) used for the main body of text of a manuscript. Use a standard and consistent nomenclature. If known, identify the scribe, notary, or corrector responsible for the production of an item. If possible, distinguish between the hands of multiple scribes, indicating the leaves upon which each worked. If the determination of dating and localization of an item has been arrived at by means of the script, identify the relevant palaeographical features. Precede this note with the heading *Script:*.

Script: Written in a chancery hand

Script: Written in medium grade, gothic book script (littera minuscula gothica textualis libraria)

Script: Written in insular phase II half-uncial, with interlinear Old English gloss in Anglo-Saxon pointed minuscule

Script: Written by 3 scribes in an early Anglicana book script (Anglicana formata): scribe 1, fol. 1r–75v; scribe 2, fol. 75v–140r; scribe 3, fol. 140r–210v

7B10. Decoration

Describe the decorative features of an item to whatever degree and level is deemed appropriate. At a minimum, give notice of the presence of illumination. Generally, describe initials and miniatures in terms of the number of lines of text or space on the page they occupy. The pattern of the description should generally begin with the most complex or elaborate decoration and follow a descending order to the most simple. Provide overall artistic commentary, if desired, following the statement of decoration. If known, identify the artist(s) or workshop responsible for the decoration of a manuscript. Precede this note with the heading *Decoration:*.[26]

In general, follow the hierarchy set out below in ordering the description.[27] Prominence of one or other elements of the decoration, however, may give these elements precedence in the order of description:

---

26. Useful guides to technical terminology in describing the decorative elements of a manuscript are: Pilar Ostos, et al., *Vocabulario codicología*, Instrumenta bibliológica (Madrid: Arcos Libros, 1997); Marilena Maniaci, *Terminologia del libro manoscritto*, Addenda: studi sulla conoscenza la conservazione e il restauro del material librario, 3 (Roma: Istituto centrale per la patologia del libro, 1996); Michelle P. Brown, *Understanding Illuminated Manuscripts: A Guide to Technical Terms* (Malibu, Calif.: J. Paul Getty Museum; London: British Library, 1994); École des hautes études en sciences sociales, Paris. Groupe d'anthropologie historique de l'Occident médiéval, *Thésaurus des images médiévales pour la constitution de bases de données iconographiques* (Paris: Centre de recherches historiques; École des hautes études en sciences sociales, 1993); Christine Jakobi, *Buchmalerei: Ihre Terminologie in der Kunstgeschichte* (Berlin: Dietrich Reimer, 1991); Denis Muzerelle, *Vocabulaire codicologique: Répertoire méthodique des termes français relatifs aux manuscrits*, Rubricae, 1 (Paris: CEMI, 1985); François Garnier, *Thesaurus iconographique: Système descriptif des représetations*, (Paris: Le Léopard d'Or, 1984); François Garnier, *Le Langage de l'image au Moyen Âge*, 2 vols. (Paris: Le Léopard d'Or, 1982); and Lucia N. Valentine, *Ornament in Medieval Manuscripts: A Glossary* (London: Faber and Faber, 1965).

27. This hierarchy is derived from Lilian M. C. Randall, *Medieval and Renaissance Manuscripts in the Walters Art Gallery*,

canon tables / calendars / carpet pages / evangelist, author, and donor portraits / miniatures / other illustrations / historiated, inhabited, anthropomorphic, zoomorphic, and zoo-anthropomorphic initials / decorated, illuminated, and painted initials / pen-flourished and penwork initials / ornamented, painted, and flourished capitals / line fillers / borders / drolleries and marginal illustrations / pensprays

Decoration: Illuminated initials and ten miniatures

Decoration: Historiated initials at head of each chapter

Decoration: Pen-flourished initials throughout

Decoration: Primary (5- to 6-line) and secondary (2- to 3-line) pen-flourished initials throughout

Decoration: Historiated initials (8-line) at head of each chapter (fols. 1r, 25r, 40r, 61v, 80r)

(The following detailed example is adapted and abridged from the description of a 13th-century Parisian psalter in order to illustrate the principle of hierarchy of description in a decoration note or notes.)[28]

Decoration 1: Calendar illustrations: fol. ir, Jan. (Janus Feasting / Aquarius); fol. ivr, Feb. (Unshod man by fire holding boot / Pisces) …

Decoration 2: Historiated initials, major Psalm divisions: fol. 7r, Ps. I, B (King David playing harp in upper compartment / David beheading Goliath in lower compartment); fol. 49r, Ps. 38, D (David kneeling and pointing to eyes before enthroned Christ) …

Decoration 3: Decorated illuminated initials: (a) 4-line gold "KL" in calendar on bipartite rose and blue ground patterned in white; (b) 2-line Psalm initials, other than major divisions, alternately in rose and blue, simply patterned in white, on rectangular grounds of opposite color, in-filled with foliate- or dragon-rinceau, some incorporating head of human or beast, bird, quadruped, or hybrid, with bird or quadruped perched atop some initials.

Decoration 4: Flourished initials: (a) Psalm versal, set off: gold and blue alternately, flourished in blue and red respectively; Dominical letters "A" in calendar: blue, flourished in red.

---

3 vols (Baltimore: Johns Hopkins University Press, 1988–97), I:xxv–xxvi, and *passim*. See also "Hierarchy" in Brown, *Understanding Illumated Manuscripts*.

 28. Baltimore, Walters Art Museum, MS. W. 58. See Randall, *Walters Art Gallery*, I:51.

Decoration 5: Line-fillers: Red, gold, and blue stylized foliate or geometric patterns, regularly alternating with panels containing animate motifs in orange, copperous green, blue, rose, light brown, favorite motifs include dragons (usually holding round object in jaws), mitered or tonsured hybrids, static or running quadrupeds, fish.

Decoration 6: Marginal pen sprays, in red and blue descending diagonally across lower margins; on versos issuing at left from extension of Psalm-initial, versal, or independent head of human or beast; on rectos, typically issuing from tail or head at right end of nearest line-filler.

7B11. Music

Make notes on musical notation contained in an item to whatever degree and level is deemed appropriate.[29] At a minimum, indicate the presence of musical notation or the system of notation employed. Precede this note with the heading *Music:*. Record information on any texts of music in a contents note.

Music: Contains musical notation

Music: Contains alphabetic notation

Music: Contains neumatic notation (Hufnagel)

Music: Contains staff notation (4 line)

7B12. Binding[30]

Describe the binding of an item to whatever degree and level is deemed appropriate. At a minimum, give notice of whether the binding is contemporary with the item, later, or modern. Assign a general date to the binding if possible. If known, identify the binder(s) responsible for the binding of a manuscript. Precede this note with the heading *Binding:*.

Binding: Modern

Binding: 20th cent. Parchment wrapper

Binding: 17th cent., early. Three-quarter calf, gold tooled

---

29. For an introduction to music in the Middle Ages, see Theodore Karp, "Medieval Music in Perspective," in James M Powell, ed., *Medieval Studies: An Introduction*, 401–31.

30. For an introduction, see Graham Pollard, "Describing Medieval Bookbindings," in *Medieval Learning and Literature: Essays Presented to Richard William Hunt*, ed. J.J.G. Alexander and M.T. Gibson (Oxford: Clarendon Press, 1976), 50–65. For fuller treatment, see Léon Gilissen, *La Reliure occidentale antérieure à 1400*, Bibliologia: elementa ad librorum studia pertinentia, 1 (Turnhout: Brepols, 1983); J.A. Szirmai, *The Archaeology of Medieval Bookbinding* (Aldershot, Hants.: Ashgate, 1999).

Binding: 15th cent. Original sewing on five slit, tawed straps laced into wooden boards. Endband cords laid in grooves. Covered with white, tawed skin, blind-tooled with a St. Andrew's cross within panel borders. The covering leather is sewn around the endbands, from spine to edges, with a back-stitch. Traces of round bosses, probably brass, and of two straps and pin fastenings, the pins on the upper board.

[Shailor, *Beinecke Library*, I:37]

7B13. Accompanying materials

Make notes on any materials attached to or accompanying an item, particularly in the case of letters or legal documents which may have, or have had, seals attached.[31] When giving dimensions of seals, measure the impression left by the seal matrix. Precede this note with the heading *Accompanying Materials:*.

Accompanying materials: With 1 seal (green, oval, 2.1 x 3.2 cm.), on a tag, bearing a fleur-de-lys and the legend: "S. JOHANNIS LE ABE"

Accompanying materials: With 1 seal (red, 2.5 cm. diam.), applied, bearing a stag

Accompanying materials: With 3 tags for seals (missing)

7B14. Origin

Make notes on the origin of an item, including date, place, agency and reason for production as accurately as can be determined. Indicate basis for localization, dating, and identification, or give reference to other notes that may contain such information. Transcribe in full any colophon or other statement regarding date, place, agency, and reason for production of an item. If such a statement is already transcribed as part of a contents note, do not repeat it separately here. Give the precise folio or page reference where information is found. If known, identify the patron, donor, or recipient of a manuscript. Precede this note with the heading *Origin:*.

Origin: Written in northern France, probably first half of 13th cent. See notes on script.

Origin: Written in Paris in 1370 by Iohannes de Papeleu. "Anno Domini millesimo trecentesimo septimo decimo, hoc opus transcriptum est a Iohanne de Papeleu, clerico Parisius commoranti in vico Scriptorum, quem velit servare Deus qui est retributor omnium bonorum in secula seculorum. Amen." (fol. 506r)

[Samaran and Marichal, *Manuscrits en écriture latine*, I:171]

---

31. As guides to the description of seals, see Hilary Jenkinson, *Guide to Seals in the Public Records Office*, 2nd ed. (London: H.M.S.O., 1968); Pierre Chaplais, *English Royal Documents: King John–Henry IV, 1199–1461* (Oxford: Clarendon Press, 1971); Michel Pastoreau, *Les Sceaux*, Typologie des sources du Moyen Âge occidental, 36 (Turnout: Brepols, 1981); P. D. A. Harvey and Andrew McGuinness, *A Guide to British Medieval Seals* (Toronto: University of Toronto Press, 1996).

Origin: Produced in Paris in 1318 by Thomas de Maubeuge for Pierre Honnorez du Neuf Chastel. "[rubr.] Ci commencent les chroniques des roys de France … lesquelles Pierres Honnorez du Nuef Chastel en Normandie fist escrire et ordener en la maniere que elles sont, selonc l'ordenance des croniques de Saint Denis, a mestre Thomas de Maubeuge, demorant en rue nueve Nostre Dame de Paris, l'an de grace Nostre Seigneur MCCCXVIII." (fol. 2r)

[M.A and R.H. Rouse, "The Book Trade at the University of Paris, ca. 1250–ca. 1350" in *Authentic Witnesses*, 279]

7B15. Provenance

Make notes on the history of ownership of an item. Note all marks of ownership such as bookplates, *ex libris* and *ex dono* inscriptions, armorial bindings, etc., as well as other physical or textual evidence that contribute to establishing provenance. Provide references to sales catalogs, inventories, or other documentation as available.

Inscription and date on fol. i recto: "En Vsu et scriptura 1573." Inscription inside front cover, in hand of 16th-cent. (visible under ultraviolet light): "Dono possideo | G Selb DX [?]". Signature of "Jac. Roch" with date "20 Aprilis 1793" on fol. 1r; later inscription "Bought of Mr. Roche of Cork," probably identifiable as James Roche, 1770–1853; DNB, v. 17, p. 69. Belonged to Sir Thomas Phillipps (no. 3899; stamp and notation inside front cover; tag on spine). From the library of George Dunn of Woolley Hall near Maidenhead (1865–1912, booklabel and inscription "dbl/ G D. | May 1903" inside front cover; his sale at Sotheby's, 2 Feb. 1914, no. 1573). Two unidentified entries from sales catalog pasted inside front cover and on first flyleaf. Belonged to Henry Fletcher.

[Shailor, *Beinecke Library*, I:288–89]

7B16. Immediate source of acquisition

Record the immediate source from which an item passed into the collection of the current holding institution. Make notes on the circumstances and date of acquisition, indicating whether the item was acquired through purchase, gift, transfer, deposit, loan, etc. Provide references to sales catalogs, accession records, and other documentation as needed. This information may be withheld from public access if desired.

Gift of Mrs. Henry Fletcher, 1953

Purchased from H.P. Kraus, 1949, April 23

7B17. Former and related shelfmarks[32]

Record any shelfmark, pressmark, or other inventory mark that may have been assigned to an item in the past. Also record any past or present related shelfmark, as in the case when an item has been dismembered and its parts have been assigned separate designations in the same or other collections. Give any discussion of former or related shelfmarks in a note on provenance. Precede this note with either the heading *Former shelfmark:* or *Related shelfmark:*.

> Former shelfmark: Bury St. Edmunds, MS S.155
> *(now London, British Library, MS Cotton Tib. B.ii)*

> Former shelfmark: Phillipps MS 21975
> *(now New York, Pierpont Morgan Library, MS 652)*

> Related shelfmark: Oxford, Bodleian Library, MS. Hatton 115
> *(related to a single dismembered leaf, now Lawrence, KS, Kenneth Spenser Research Library, Pryce MS C2:2)*

7B18. Bynames

Record the byname of an item—that is, the popular name or names by which an item is or has been familiarly known, other than by the title of the work it contains or by its shelfmark.[33] If a manuscript possesses a popular name, this byname or one of its bynames will also usually be the uniform title for the manuscript (see AACR2R 25.13). Precede this note with the heading *Byname:*.

> Byname: Ellesmere Chaucer

> Byname: Medici Vergil

> Byname: Parker Chronicles and Laws

> Byname: Vienna Dioscurides

> Byname: Manesse codex; Grosse Heidelberger Liederhandschrift; Manessische Handschrift; …

7B19. Current shelfmark

Record the current shelfmark of an item using the standard form of scholarly citation. The cita-

---

32. On medieval shelfmarks and library catalogs, see Richard Sharpe, "Accession, Classification, Location: Shelfmarks in Medieval Libraries," *Scriptorium* 50 (1996): 279–87; N.R. Ker, *Medieval Libraries of Great Britain*, 2nd ed., (London: Royal Historical Society, 1964); and Albert Derolez, *Les Catalogues de bibliothèques*, Typlogie des sources du Moyen Âge occidental, 31 (Turnhout: Brepols, 1979).

33. See Wilma Fitzgerald, *Ocelli nominum: Names and Shelf Marks of Famous/Familiar Manuscripts*, Subsidia mediaevalia, 19 (Toronto: Pontifical Institute of Medieval Studies, 1992).

tion of a shelfmark normally consists of four main elements: the geographical location of the repository, the name of the repository itself, an abbreviated form of the designation manuscript (usually MS, or Ms, or ms., or Hs., or Cod., etc.) and the repository designation for the manuscript. The citation of a shelfmark must reproduce exactly any abbreviation, punctuation, use of upper and lower case letters, and any other features used by the holding institution to identify the item. The scholarly form of a shelfmark citation is distinct from the same shelfmark formulated as a uniform title (see Appendix A3.1.2 and AACR2R 25.13). Precede this note with the heading *Shelfmark:*.

Shelfmark: Oxford, Bodleian Library, MS. Douce 217

Shelfmark: Paris, Bibliothèque nationale de France, ms. fr. 10135

Shelfmark: Vienna, Österreichische Nationalbibliothek, Hs. 2564

Shelfmark: New York, Pierpont Morgan Library. MS M.1

Shelfmark: Munich, Bayerische Staatsbibliothek, Cod. Gall. 4

7B20. Reference to published descriptions or citations

Give precise references to the most authoritative and comprehensive published descriptions or standard citations for an item. Provide references constructed according to Peter M. Van Wingen, *Standard Citation Forms for Rare Book Cataloging*, 2nd ed. (Washington, D.C.: Library of Congress, Cataloging Distribution Service, 1996), xvi–xxvii. Give as many references as necessary, listing the most current, authoritative, and comprehensive items first.

E.g., for Nekcsei-Lipócz Bible (Washington, D.C., Library of Congress, Ms. BS75 1335)

Schutzner, S. Med. and Ren. bks. in LC, I, 6
   Svato Schutzner, Medieval and Renaissance Manuscript Books in the Library of Congress: A Descriptive Catalog, 2 vols. (Washington, D.C.: Library of Congress, 1989–)

De Ricci, p. 180, no. 1
   Seymour de Ricci, Census of Medieval and Renaissance Manuscripts in the United States and Canada, 3 vols. (New York: H.W. Wilson, 1935–40)

Fay & Bond, p. 117, no. 1
   C.U. Faye, Supplement to the Census of Medieval and Renaissance Manuscripts in the United States and Canada, ed. W.H. Bond (New York: Bibliographical Society of America, 1962)

7B21. Reference to published editions, facsimiles, or treatments

Give precise references to the most authoritative and comprehensive published text editions, facsimile reproductions, monographic studies, or articles on an item. References may be to the work or to the physical item or to both. Provide references constructed according to 7B20. Give as many references as necessary, listing the most current, authoritative, and comprehensive items first.

> PL, 103, cols. 485–554
>> *Patrologiae cursus completus, series latina*, ed. J.-P. Migne, 221 vols. (Paris, 1844–64)

> Hunter Blair, P. Moore Bede. Early English mss in facsimile, 9
>> Peter Hunter Blair, *The Moore Bede: An Eighth-Century Manuscript of the Venerable Bede's Historia ecclesiastica gentis Anglorum in Cambridge University Library (Kk.5.16)*, Early English Manuscripts in Facsimile, 9 (Copenhagen: Rosenkilde and Bagger, 1959)

> Hamburger, J.F. Rothschild canticles
>> Jeffrey F. Hamburger, *The Rothschild Canticles: Art and Mysticism in Flanders and the Rhineland circa 1300* (New Haven: Yale University Press, 1990)

7B22. Additional physical form

If desired, provide information on any reproductions, transcriptions, or other additional physical or electronic formats in which an original item may exist, either for use at the holding institution, through remote access, or in published form. Include notes on the extent to which an original item or the work(s) it contains is reproduced.

> Also available in microfilm: for use in library only

> Also available in CD ROM (illuminations only)

> Also available in digital format: accessible through library website

> Partial transcription of text (paper: 20th cent.): for use in library only

7B23. Form of reproduction

Record information describing an item that is a reproduction of an original (*e.g.*, microfilm) when cataloging from a reproduction and when information in the bibliographic record represents the original. Indicate the type, place, agency, date, physical description, series statement, publication, and extent of the reproduction (when not complete) as applicable. Include a statement of reproduction in every catalog record associated with a reproduced item being described (*i.e.*, in both the host item and analytic records when applicable).

> Microfilm. Vatican City : Biblioteca Apostolica Vaticana, 1958. 1 microfilm reel ; 35 mm.

> Microfiche. Binghamton, N.Y. : Medieval & Renaissance Texts & Studies, 1994– . 1 microfiche; (Anglo-Saxon Manuscripts in Microfiche Facsimile, ASM 1.1 ; Medieval & Renaissance Texts & Studies, 136–37)

7B24. Restrictions on access

If desired, record any special circumstance affecting access to material, such as restrictions of gift or bequest, special permissions required, restricted locality for use, or fragile condition. State whether it is preferable that a substitute physical form of the item be consulted in place of the original, such as a printed facsimile or a microform or digital reproduction.

> Access limited: Use of reproduction preferred

> Access restricted: Apply to curator of manuscripts

> Available for consultation in East Reading Room only

7B25. Terms governing use and reproduction

If desired, record conditions governing use and reproduction of material once access has been obtained. Indicate limitations on use of content of material and conditions affecting reproduction.

> Apply for permission to publish

> Reproduction limited by copyright

> Digital images protected by copyright

7B26. Location of originals / reproductions

If desired, record the name and location of the repository with custody over originals or reproductions of an item or items being described.

> *Original*
> Biblioteca Apostolica Vaticana; Vatican City

> *Reproduction*
> Microfilm Knights of Columbus Vatican Film Library, Pius XII Memorial Library,
>   Saint Louis University; 3650 Lindell Boulevard, St. Louis, MO 63108; USA;
>   314-977-3090

7B27. Cataloging history

Record here details concerning the origin of the content of an item description. At a minimum, indicate whether an item description is the product of original cataloging from an item in hand or from a reproduction, or whether an item description is provided from a previously existing item description (printed or handwritten), and indicate the date of an item description. Indicate revisions or additions to an item description following any earlier cataloging history. If desired, also record the name of the individual responsible for the content of an item description.

Item cataloged in hand by [*name of cataloger*], [date]

Item cataloged from microform reproduction by [*name of cataloger*], [date]

Item cataloged from existing description: [*reference to published or unpublished description*]

Item cataloged in hand by [*name of cataloger*], [*date*]; revised by [*name of cataloger*], [*date*]; decoration description provided by [*name of cataloger*], [*date*] …

8. STANDARD NUMBER AND TERMS OF AVAILABILITY AREA

8A
This area is not used for manuscripts.

APPENDIX A:
ADDED ENTRY ACCESS

Contents

A1. General rule

Follow the general rules as provided in *AACR2R* 21.29.

A2. Specific rules

Follow the specific rules as provided in *AACR2R* 21.30, with the following additions or modifications given below.

A2.1. Two or more persons or corporate bodies involved

If two or more persons or corporate bodies are involved in the creation, translation, or editing of a work, or in the production of an item, make added entries under the headings for all persons or corporate bodies involved not given as the main entry. In cases where large numbers of persons or corporate bodies are involved, make added entries for as many persons or corporate bodies as practicable or that are deemed significant.

A2.2. Analytical added entries

If two or more works contained in an item being cataloged are not given separate analysis, make analytical added entries under the appropriate title or author-title headings for all significant authors and titles of works (as determined by the cataloger) not given as the main entry.

A2.3. Title added entry access

Title added entry access may be desirable in certain instances when access through variations or permutations of the title proper, alternate title, parallel title, or other title information will better facilitate the retrieval of an item. Titles given to works in manuscript can be highly variable from one copy to another and, thus, be unpredictable, thereby diminishing the value of the transcribed title both as a means of direct access and as a device for collocation of multiple copies. More frequently it will be through the uniform title of the work or the manuscript (see Appendix A3.1.2) that access will be sought. However, within families of manuscripts or among certain common works there may be a degree of commonality in the titles that will make increased title access desirable. A normalized or classicized form of orthographic irregularities might also facilitate increased access.

Make title added entries for variations of the title proper that are deemed significant and useful for increased access. The recommendations below should be applied at the discretion of the cataloger as appropriate to the item in hand.

General provision
Make an added entry for the title proper as it has been transcribed, omitting only an initial article as required. If the title proper is lengthy, make a shortened added entry that ends at the first logical point after the fifth word. Make added entries for significant variations of the title proper, such as might appear in colophons, running titles, spine titles, cover titles, etc.

0F5. Variantly and erroneously spelled words
Make an added entry for the title proper using corrected and normalized spelling of words variantly or erroneously spelled, declined, or conjugated. In the case of Latin texts, provide classical spellings. In the case of vernacular texts, provide the normalized contemporary spellings (*i.e.*, do not modernize the spelling of a pre-modern vernacular languages, such as rendering an Old French text in modern French spelling).

0F6. Missing letters and illegible text
Make an added entry for a title supplying missing letters and illegible text without sign of editorial intervention.

0F7. Manuscript corrections
If manuscript corrections have been incorporated as part of a title, make an added entry for the title in its uncorrected state, if desired.

0F8. Abbreviations
Make an added entry for a title expanding fully all abbreviations without sign of

editorial intervention. Unless considered necessary, do not make an added entry for a title preserving the abbreviations in an unexpanded form.

1B1. Title proper

1B1.4. Items lacking a collective title
Make added entries for titles other than the first transcribed as part of a collective title proper.

7B4. Variations of title and statement of responsibility

A3. ADDED ENTRIES REQUIRED IN THE CATALOG RECORD
The following added entries required in the catalog record define only a minimum set of added entries for each level of description. Added entry access may be selectively augmented according to local cataloging policies. For instance, an institution choosing to create summary descriptions for its holdings may also desire to provide added entry access for former shelfmarks, such as is normally given in a detailed description. In all cases, information is supplied on the basis of its availability and applicability.

A3.1. Added entries required in a summary description
A summary description requires at least the added entries listed below to be included in the catalog record, if the information is available and applicable.

A3.1.1. Place of production (4C, 7B14)
Make a hierarchical added entry for the place of production of an item, giving the country, significant area subdivisions, and specific place. Use modern established forms for place-names and geo-political boundaries. If these names or boundaries have changed since the date of creation of an item, give the modern established forms for both the place-names and the original and modern boundaries.

France – Normandy – Rouen

Belgium – Flanders – Ghent

Italy – Rome

Spain – Catalonia

A3.1.2. Uniform title of the manuscript
Make an added entry for the uniform title of a manuscript as a physical entity, following the provisions of *AACR2R* 25.13 and the related Library of Congress Rule Interpretation.

Manuscripts usually possess two uniform titles, one for the work contained in the manuscript and one for the manuscript itself as a physical entity. While a manuscript as a physical entity will have only a single uniform title, the source for this title will either be the byname or popular name of the manuscript, if such a name exists, and in which case there may be multiple such names (see 7B18), or the shelfmark of the manuscript. An authority structure should exist or be created to resolve all cross-references. Regardless of whether an original manuscript or its reproduction is being cataloged, main entry access is given through the work.

> *For the manuscript copy of the Canterbury Tales by Geoffrey Chaucer popularly known as the Ellesmere Chaucer and housed in the Huntington Library in San Marino, California, as MS EL 26 C 9:*
>
> **Main entry under**: *Chaucer, Geoffrey, d. 1400*
> **Uniform title**: *Canterbury tales*
> **Byname**: *Ellesmere Chaucer*
> **Shelfmark**: *San Marino, CA, Henry E. Huntington Library, MS EL 26 C 9*
> **Added entry under uniform title**: *Ellesmere Chaucer*

Only in the case of a work that exists in a unique manuscript copy will the uniform title for the work and the manuscript as a physical entity be the same.

> *For the anonymous Mixtec manuscript showing in picture and hieroglyph the succession and genealogy of kings in pre-Conquest southern Mexico popularly known variously as the Codex Nuttall or Codex Zouche or Codex Zouche-Nuttall and housed in the British Library in London as MS Additional 39671:*
>
> **Main entry under uniform title**: *Codex Nuttall*
> **Byname**: *Codex Nuttal, Codex Zouche, Codex Zouche-Nuttall*
> **Shelfmark**: *London, British Library, MS Additional 39671*

For manuscripts of sacred scripture or liturgical works an abbreviated form of the uniform title of the manuscript as a physical entity (either the byname or the shelfmark) is recorded as an addition to the uniform title for the work (see *AACR2R 25.18A12 and 25.22B*).

> **Main entry under**: *Catholic Church*
> **Uniform title**: *Book of hours (Ms. De Brailes)*
> **Byname**: *William de Brailes hours; De Brailes hours*
> **Shelfmark**: *London, British Library, MS Additional 49999*
> **Added entry under uniform title**: *De Brailes hours*
>
> **Main entry under**: *Catholic Church*
> **Uniform title**: *Book of hours (Ms. Honnold Library. Crispin 20)*
> **Shelfmark**: *Claremont, CA, Honnold Library, MS Crispin 20*

Added entry under uniform title: Honnold Library for the Associated Colleges. Manuscript. Crispin 20

Main entry under: Catholic Church
Uniform title: Psalter (Ms. Blanche of Castile)
Byname: St. Louis and Blanche of Castile psalter; Blanche of Castile psalter; Royal psalter
Shelfmark: Paris, Bibliothèque de l'Arsenal, ms. 1186
Added entry under uniform title: Blanche of Castile psalter

Main entry under uniform title: Haggadah (Ms. Rylands)
Byname: Rylands haggadah, Rylands Spanish haggadah, Ryland Sephardi haggadah
Shelfmark: Manchester, John Rylands Library, MS Heb. 6
Added entry under uniform title: Rylands haggadah

Main entry under uniform title: Bible. N.T. Revelation. Latin. Trinity apocalypse
Byname: Trinity apocalypse; Trinity College apocalypse
Shelfmark: Cambridge, Trinity College, MS 950 (R.16.2)
Added entry under uniform title: Trinity apocalypse

Formulate a shelfmark as a uniform title according to *AACR2R* 25.13B1c. Do not repeat terms such as "manuscript," "codex," etc. or their abbreviations as part of the repository designation, unless these terms constitute essential or integral elements of the repository designation. A shelfmark is formulated differently in the notes (see 7B19) from the shelfmark as a uniform title. When applicable, include the foliation or pagination for the leaves occupied by the work being described.

Henry E. Huntington Library and Art Gallery. Manuscript. BA 29

British Library. Manuscript. Cotton Otho A. XII

Biblioteca apostolica vaticana. Manuscript. Vat. lat. 679

Corpus Christi College (University of Cambridge). Library. Manuscript. 173, fol. 1r–56r

A3.2. Added entries required in a detailed description
A detailed description requires at least the added entries listed below, in addition to those listed in A3.1, to be included in the catalog record, if the information is available and applicable.

A3.2.1. Secundo folio (7B6)
Make an added entry for the secundo folio reference of a literary, legal, medical, scientific work, etc., but not for letters, legal documents, or archival records, owned in the Middle Ages by a corporate body. Identify this added entry with the designation "Secundo folio" followed by a colon.

A3.2.2. Names associated with production and ownership (7B14–15)

Make added entries for all persons, families, or corporate bodies associated with the production and ownership of an item.

APPENDIX B: ANALYSIS

Contents

B1. ANALYSIS

Separate analysis of constituent works contained in a manuscript codex or in a composite manuscript codex is required for detailed descriptions when applicable. Create catalog records for a composite manuscript codex using an analytic structure (see *AACR2R* 13.5) consisting of a host item record for the codex itself and multiple analytic constituent records for individually analyzed works. Do not give separate analysis for the constituent parts of standard works whose contents vary within a defined set of texts (*e.g.*, the Bible or liturgical and devotional works) or for compiled works (*e.g.*, collections of sermons, hymns, letters, laws and statutes, charter, writs, and other legal documents, etc.), unless this is deemed desirable. Separate analysis for constituent works in a composite manuscript codex is not required when providing only a summary description, but it may be used if desired.

A manuscript codex or composite manuscript codex containing multiple works that were originally produced as a unit or later bound together do not require the addition of a "Bound with" note in either the host item or constituent works record. This information is indicated either through the contents note (which in all cases is required to be complete) or through a host item linking entry (see below).

B2. LINKING ENTRIES REQUIRED IN THE CATALOG RECORD

If an analytic structure is used to describe a host item and its constituent works, provide a host item linking entry in each of the analytic records for the constituent works to indicate the subordinate relationship of the analytic records to their host item. If desired, constituent unit linking entries may also be provided in the host item record to indicate the reciprocal relationship of the host item to its analytic records. However, constituent unit linking entries may not be used as a substitute for the contents note in the host item record.

B3. DISTRIBUTION OF ELEMENTS BETWEEN HOST ITEM AND ANALYTIC CATALOG RECORDS

Distribute descriptive information, added entries, and subject analysis between host item and analytic catalog records according to the policies of the cataloging institution. A basic set of descriptive elements is required and common to all records (host item and analytic) regardless of level of description (see 0D). However, the principal that should guide the distribution of notes, added entries, and subject analysis between host item and analytic records is the appropriateness of this information and these access points to the host item as a whole or to the individual constituent work. The result is that some information is normally provided only in the host item record (*e.g.,* Statement of Collation); some information is duplicated in both the host item record and its analytic constituent records (*e.g.,* Form of Reproduction); some categories of information are repeated in both the host item record and its analytic constituent records, but contain synoptic information appropriate to the whole in one and specific information appropriate to the constituent work in the other (*e.g.,* Contents); and some information is normally provided only in the analytic constituent record (*e.g.,* Host Item Linking Entry). Particular circumstances, however, may affect the normal distribution of information, placing information normally provided in the host item record instead in the analytic constituent record (*e.g.,* Script or Decoration particular to an individual work meriting separate treatment).

Elements normally **common** *to host item and analytic records:*

1. TITLE AND STATEMENT OF RESPONSIBILITY
    Title proper
    General material designation (*optional*)
    Parallel title
    Other title information
    First and subsequent statements of responsibility
2. EDITION/VERSION
    Statement of edition / version
    Statement of responsibility relating to edition / version
4. PLACE AND DATE OF PRODUCTION
5. PHYSICAL DESCRIPTION
    Extent
    Other physical details
    Dimensions
7. NOTES
    7B1.   Format, nature, and scope
    7B2.   Language
    7B3.   Source of title and statement of responsibility
    7B4.   Variations of title and statement of responsibility
    7B5.   Contents
    7B17. Former and related shelfmarks
    7B19. Current shelfmark
    7B20. Reference to published descriptions or citations
    7B21. Reference to published editions, facsimiles, or treatments
    7B23. Form of reproduction
    7B27. Cataloging history

APPENDIX A. ADDED ENTRY ACCESS POINTS
  A3.1.1. Place of production
  A3.1.2. Uniform title of the manuscript

*Elements normally found **only** in host item record:*

7. NOTES
  7B6. Secundo folio
  7B7. Statement of collation
  7B8. Layout
  7B9. Script
  7B10. Decoration
  7B11. Music
  7B12. Binding
  7B14. Origin
  7B15. Provenance
  7B16. Immediate source of acquisition
  7B18. Bynames
  7B24. Restrictions on access
  7B25. Terms governing use and reproduction

Genre/form analysis
APPENDIX A. ADDED ENTRY ACCESS
        POINTS
  A3.2.2. Secundo folio
  A3.2.3. Names associated with production and
        ownership
APPENDIX B. ANALYSIS
    B2. Constituent unit linking entries

*Elements normally found **only** in analytic record:*

Subject analysis
APPENDIX B. ANALYSIS
      B2. Host item linking entry

APPENDIX C:
MARC 21 CODING SUMMARY
AND EXAMPLES

MARC 21 CODING SUMMARY

The following list of MARC 21 leaders, control fields, and tags represents only those most commonly used or those that are required in constructing an AMREMM catalog record. It does not define the complete set of leaders, control fields, and tags that may be used.

Leader / Control Field / Tag	Codes / Elements / Notes / Added Entries
Leader 06 (type of record)	*t (manuscript language material)*
Leader 07 (bibliographic level)	*a (monographic component part)*
	c (collection)
	m (monograph/item)
Leader 08 (type of control)	*– (Do not use code "a" for archival control. AMREMM provides bibliographical control over manuscript materials)*
Leader 17 (encoding level)	*– (full level: summary and detailed levels of description correspond to full-level cataloging, regardless of whether an original or reproduction is used as the basis for the description)*
	1 (full level, material not examined: use when an item is cataloged exclusively from a previously existing manuscript description)
Leader 18 (descriptive cataloging form)	*a (AACR2)*
Control field 007/00 (category of material)	*c (computer file)*
	h (microform)
Control field 008/06 (type of date)	*i (inclusive dates of a collection: e.g., 1420–1500)*
	k (range of years of bulk collection: e.g., 1430–1460)
	q (questionable date: e.g., 1415?–1460, between 11–– and 12––, between 11––? and 12––?, between 1100 and 1125, between 1125 and 1150, etc.)

	s (single known date/probable date: e.g., 1215, 1215?,
	ca. 1349, ca. 1349?, 112–, 112–?, 11––, 11––?)
Control field 008/15–17 (place of production)	*e.g., fr, enk*
Control field 008/18–21 (illustrations)	*– (no illustrations)*
	a (illustrations)
	p (illuminations)
Control field 008/35–37 (language)	*e.g., lat, eng, etc.*
040 ‡e	*amremm*
041	*e.g., englat*
1xx	*main entry heading*
240	*uniform title*
245	*title and statement of responsibility*
246 ‡i [fol. ref.]: ‡a	*variations of title*
246 ‡i Secundo folio: ‡a	*secundo folio*
250	*edition / version*
260 ‡a	*place of production*
260 ‡c	*date of production*
300 ‡a	*extent*
300 ‡b	*support*
300 ‡b	*decoration*
300 ‡c	*dimensions*
300 ‡e	*accompanying materials*
500	*format (see below nature and scope)*
500	*source of title and statement of responsibility*
500‡a Collation:	*statement of collation*
500‡a Layout:	*layout*
500‡a Script:	*script*
500‡a Decoration:	*decoration*
500‡a Binding:	*binding*
500‡a Accompanying materials:	*accompanying materials*
500‡a Origin:	*origin*
500‡a Former shelfmark:	*former shelfmark*
500‡a Related shelfmark:	*related shelfmark*
500‡a Byname:	*byname*
500‡a Shelfmark:	*current shelfmark*
505	*contents*
506	*restrictions on access*
510	*reference to published descriptions or citations*
520	*nature and scope (see above format)*
530	*additional physical form*
533	*form of reproduction*
535	*location of originals/reproductions*

540	*terms governing use and reproduction*
541	*immediate source of acquisition*
546	*language*
561	*provenance*
581	*reference to published editions, facsimiles, or treatments*
583 ‡z	*cataloging history*
6xx	*subject headings as applicable*
655	*form/genre headings as applicable*
7xx	*added entry headings as applicable*
700	*name of agency of production—individual*
700 ‡e former owner	*former owner—individual*
700 ‡e scribe	*scribe*
700 ‡e corrector	*corrector*
700 ‡e artist	*artist*
700 ‡e illuminator	*illuminator*
700 ‡e rubricator	*rubricator*
700 ‡e binder	*binder*
700 ‡e donor	*donor*
700 ‡e patron	*patron*
710 *or* 730	*uniform title of manuscript*
710	*name of agency of production—corporate body*
710 ‡e former owner	*former owner—corporate body*
730 *or* 710	*uniform title of manuscript*
740	*added entry—uncontrolled related/analytical title as applicable*
752	*place of production*
773	*host item linking entry*
774	*constituent unit linking entry*
776	*additional physical form*

MARC 21 CODING EXAMPLES

1. TITLE AND STATEMENT OF RESPONSIBILITY AREA

1A2.2

245:10: ‡a P[ublii] Vergilii Mar[onis] Bucolicorum liber.

245:10: ‡a Speculum iudiciale / ‡c a Magistro Guillelmo Duranti compositum.

245:10: ‡a Commentariorum C[aii] Iulii Caesaris de bello Gallico liber ‡c / Iulius Celsus Constantinus quintus consul emendavit.

245:10: ‡a Marcrobii Theodosii viri illustrissimi Saturnalium liber.

245:00: ‡a Modus quomodo parliamentum regis Anglie et Anglorum suorum tenebatur.

245:00: ‡a Vita et passio S[ancte] Thome Cantuariensis Archiepiscopi et Martyris.

245:10: ‡a Liber ethicorum / ‡c compilatus a Fratre Alberto Theutonico de Ordine Fratrum Predicatorum.

245:10: ‡a Politicorum Aristotelis liber.

245:10: ‡a Sancti Ambrosii Episcopi De officiis ministrorum.

245:10: ‡a Pour se que pluisours gens desirent asavoir la nature des faucons.

245:13: ‡a La nature des faucons.

245:10: ‡a Des faucons.

245:10: ‡a Des oysiaus.

245:10: ‡a [Traité de la fauconnerie].

1B1.1

245:13: ‡a Le rommant de la rose.

245:10: ‡a Hystoria Brittonum.

245:10: ‡a Actas de las cortes de Madrid año 1393.

245:10: ‡a Regula Sancti Benedicti.

245:10: ‡a Petri Lombardi Sententiarum IV.

245:10: ‡a Sermo Beati Augustini Episcopi de nativitate Domini.

245:10: ‡a Commentarii et expositione Georgii Trapezuntii in aphorismis libri fructus Ptolomei.

245:10: ‡a Periphyseon, id est, De divisione naturae.

245:10: ‡a Liber physicorum, sive, Auditus physici.

245:10: ‡a Consulta Beati Basilii, que dicuntur, Regula eiusdem.

1B1.2

245:10: ‡a [Questiones disputate Sancti Thome]

1B1.4

245:10: ‡a Carta foreste … [etc.].

245:10: ‡a Epistole Ivonis Carnotensis Episcopi … [etc.].

1B1.5

245:10: ‡a Scriptum Ethicorum Aristotelis / ‡c secundum Thomam de Aquino. Super libro Rhetoricorum Aristotelis / editum a Fratre Egidio de Roma.

245:10: ‡a Aurelii Augustini Doctoris De sermone Domini in monte ; ‡b Sancti Augustini In epistolam Sancti Iohannis Apostoli. Sancti Ambrosii Episcopi De officiis ministrorum.

245:10: ‡a Hystoria evangelium. ‡b Hystoria actuum apostolorum … [etc.].

1B1.6

245:10: ‡a [De consolatione philosphiae].

245:10: ‡a [Historia regum Britanniae].

245:00: ‡a [Bestiary].

245:00: ‡a [Herbal].

110:2–: ‡a Catholic Church.
240:10: ‡a Book of hours (Ms. National Art Library. MSL/1902/1654)
245:10: ‡a [Book of hours : ‡b use of Rouen].
710:2–: ‡a National Art Library (Great Britain). ‡k Manuscript. ‡n MSL/1902/1654.

110:2–: ‡a Catholic Church.
240:10: ‡a Psalter (Ms. Library of Congress. BX2033.A2 1200z)
245:10: ‡a [Psalter].
710:2–: ‡a Library of Congress. ‡k Manuscript. ‡n BX2033.A2 1200z.

110:2–: ‡a Catholic Church.
240:10: ‡a Psalter (Ms. Utrecht)

245:10: ‡a [Psalter].
730:0–: ‡a Utrecht psalter.

130:0–: ‡a Bible. ‡p N.T. ‡p Acts of the Apostles. ‡l Coptic. ‡s Pierpont Morgan
    Library. ‡k Manuscript. ‡n G.67
245:10: ‡a [Acts of the Apostles].
710:2–: ‡a Pierpont Morgan Library. ‡k Manuscript. ‡n. G.67.

130:0–: ‡a Bible. ‡p N.T. ‡p Revelation. ‡l Latin. ‡s British Library. ‡k Manuscript.
    ‡n Royal 19 B. xv.
245:10: ‡a [Apocalypse].
710:2–: ‡a British Library. ‡k Manuscript. ‡n. Royal 19 B. xv.

130:0–: ‡a Bible. ‡p N.T. ‡p Psalms. ‡l Latin. ‡s Houghton Library. ‡k Manuscript.
    ‡n MS Typ 260.
245:10: ‡a [Psalms : ‡b with Glossa ordinaria].
730:02: ‡a Glossa ordinaria.
710:2–: ‡a Houghton Library. ‡k Manuscript. ‡n MS Typ 260.

100:0–: ‡a Gilbert, ‡c de La Porrée, Bishop, ‡d ca. 1075–1154.
245:10: ‡a [Commentarius in Psalmos].
730:02: ‡a Bible. ‡N.T. ‡p Psalms. ‡l Latin. ‡s Houghton Library. ‡k Manuscript.
    ‡n fMS Typ 29.
710:2–: ‡a Houghton Library. ‡k Manuscript. ‡n fMS Typ 29.

245:00: ‡a [Treatises on rhetoric].

245:00: ‡a [Arthurian romances].

245:00: ‡a [Florilegium].

245:00: ‡a [Medical formulary].

245:00: ‡a [Sermons].

110:1–: ‡a Great Britain.
240:10: ‡a Laws, etc.
245:10: ‡a [Commonplace book of legal precedents].

110:1–: ‡a Great Britain.
240:10: ‡a Laws, etc. (Year books : 5–7 Edward III)
245:10: ‡a [Year books : ‡b 5–7 Edward III].

110:1–: ‡a Great Britain.
240:10: ‡a Laws, etc. (Statuta nova : 1 Edward III – 23 Henry VI)
245:10: ‡a [Statuta nova : ‡b 1 Edward III – 23 Henry VI].

1B2.2

245:10: ‡a [Letter, 1533 Sept. 26, Waltham Abbey to Arthur Plantagenet, Lord Lisle, Calais].

245:10: ‡a [Letter, 1454(?) Feb. 1, Norwich to John Paston I].

245:10: ‡a [Letters, 1452–1510].

245:10: ‡a [Letters, 1555–1635 (bulk 1590–1610)].

1B2.3

245:10: ‡a [Grant, 1325 June 26, of land in Hooke (Dorset) to John de Barkingdon].

245:10: ‡a [Lease, 1586 June 10, of the manor of White Waltham (Berks.) to Thomas Grove].

245:10: ‡a [Quitclaim, 1290 June 27, of rights in the manor of Washfield (Devon) to Henry le Abbe].

245:10: ‡a [Marriage settlement, 1665 April 20, between Alice Meredith Croft and John Maende].

245:00: ‡a [Writs, 1356–1642].

245:00: ‡a [Manor rolls, 1282–1419 (bulk 1350–1419)].

245:10: ‡a [Cartulary, 955–1316].

245:00: ‡a [Register of writs, 1285–1415].

245:10: ‡a [Mercantile records, 1476-1502 (bulk 1495–1502)].

1E1

245:10: ‡a Regula Beati Francisci : ‡b confirmata a domino Pape Honorio.

245:10: ‡a Officium Beate Marie Virginis : ‡b secundum consuetudinem Romane curie.

245:14: ‡a The inventarye of all the goodes and chattells of John Edolf, late of New Romnye, gent., deceased : ‡b taken and priced the xx. daie of Septemb[e]r 1576 in the xviii. yere of the raigne of o[u]r soveraign ladye Quene Elisabeth.

245:12: ‡a L'ordre [et] police gardez en l'institution de l'Appotiquairerye, College [et] Chapelle de la Charité Chrestienne : ‡b pour les pauvres honteux, prestres, escoliers, gentilzhommes, marchans [et] artisans de la ville [et] faulxbourgs de Paris, detenus en extremite de maladie/‡c de l'invention de Nicolas Houël, Parisien.

1E2

245:10: ‡a Propheta magnus surrexit : ‡b [sermon on Luke XIV, 10].

1F1

245:10: ‡a Legenda aurea / ‡c de Iocabo de Voragine.

245:10: ‡a Marci Catonis vita / ‡c per Leonardum Arretinum e Plutarcho in Latinum traducta.

245:13: ‡a Le livre des proprietes des choses / ‡c translate de Latin en Francois l'an mil trois cens sexante et douze par le commandement du Roy Charles le quint de son nom regnant en France noblement et puissaument en ce temps.

245:10: ‡a Cassiodori Senatoris De institutionibus divinarum litterarum.

245:10: ‡a Additiones domini Prioris Petri super Regula Sancti Salvatoris.

245:10: ‡a Liber … historie gentis Anglorum.

1F2

245:10: ‡a Rationale divinorum officiorum / ‡c [Wilelmus Durhant].

1F4

245:10: ‡a Della nobilita civile / ‡c de M. Girolamo Osorio ; Portoghese tradotta in lingua Italiana de Bernado Trivigiano.

1F5

245:10: ‡a Liber dyalogorum Beati Gregorii Pape Doctoris.

245:10: ‡a Anicii Manlii Severini Boetii viri illustris et consularis ordinarii patricii Liber de consolatione philosophie.

245:10: ‡a De regimine principum / ‡c editus a Fratre Egidio Romano Ordinis Fratrum Heremitarum Sancti Augustini.

245:13: ‡a La controversie de noblesse plaidoyee entre Publius Cornelius Scipion dune part et Gaius Flaminius de aultre part/‡c laquelle a este faicte et composee par un notable docteur en loix et grant orateur nomme Surse de Pistoye'.

2. EDITION/VERSION AREA

2B2

250:--: ‡a Versio ultima.

4. PLACE AND DATE OF PRODUCTION AREA

4C1

260:--: ‡a [Spain]

260:--: ‡a [France]

260:--: ‡a [Brittany]

260:--: ‡a [Osnabrück]

260:--: ‡a Paris.

4C2

260:--: ‡a [England?]

260:--: ‡a [Siena?]

4D1

260:--: ‡c [1399]

260:--: ‡c [1271]

260:--: ‡c [1455]

260:--: ‡c 1474.

4D2

260:--: ‡c [1215?]

260:--: ‡c [ca. 1350]

260:--: ‡c [ca. 1350?]

260:--: ‡c [1415?–1460]

260:--: ‡c [112–]

260:--: ‡c [112–?]

260:--: ‡c [11--]

260:--: ‡c [11--?]

260:--: ‡c [between 11-- and 12--]

260:--: ‡c [between 11--? and 12--?]

260:--: ‡c [between 1100 and 1125]

260:--: ‡c [between 1125 and 1150]

260:--: ‡c [between 1100 and 1150]

260:--: ‡c [between 1125 and 1175]

260:--: ‡c [between 1150 and 1199]

260:--: ‡c [between 1150 and 1175]

260:--: ‡c [between 1175 and 1199]

260:--: ‡c [between 1175 and 1225]

5. PHYSICAL DESCRIPTION AREA

5B2

300:--: ‡a 1 leaf.

300:--: ‡a 1 bifolium.

300:--: ‡a 125 leaves.

300:––: ‡a 2 sheets.

300:––: ‡a 1 roll (5 sheets)

300:––: ‡a 1 roll (8 membranes)

300:––: ‡a 1 item.

5B3

300:––: ‡a leaves 5r–30v.

300:––: ‡a leaves 1r–26v, 26r [bis]

300:––: ‡a p. 10–15.

5B4

300:––: ‡a 2 v. (200, 150 leaves)

300:––: ‡a 3 rolls (8, 5, 10 sheets)

5B5

300:––: ‡a 83 items.

5C1

300:––: ‡a 20 leaves : ‡b parchment.

300:––: ‡a 15 leaves : ‡b paper.

300:––: ‡a 7 leaves : ‡b papyrus.

300:––: ‡a 1 sheet : ‡ parchment.

300:––: ‡a 1 roll (10 sheets) : ‡b parchment.

300:––: ‡a 1 roll (5 sheets) : ‡b paper.

300:––: ‡a 1 roll : ‡b papyrus.

5C2

300:––: ‡a 93 leaves : ‡b parchment, ill.

300:––: ‡a 60 leaves : ‡b parchment, ill., 2 maps.

5D1

> 300:--: ‡a 60 leaves : ‡b parchment ; ‡c 254 x 171 (209 x 121) mm. bound to 259 x 176 mm.

> 300:--: ‡a 95 leaves : ‡b parchment ; ‡c 236–246 x 176 (190 x 132) mm. bound to 253 x 183 mm.

5D2

> 300:--: ‡a 10 leaves : ‡b parchment ; ‡c 200 x 150 (160) mm. bound to 210 x 160 mm.

5D3

> 300:--: ‡a 1 sheet : ‡b parchment ; ‡c 230 x 380 mm.

5D4

> 300:--: ‡a 1 roll (10 sheets) : ‡b parchment ; ‡c 3000 x 300 mm.

> 300:--: ‡a 1 roll (4 sheets) : ‡b paper ; ‡c 1200 x 300 mm.

5E1

> 300:--: ‡a 1 sheet : ‡b parchment ; ‡c 160 x 300 mm. + ‡e 2 seals.

7. NOTE AREA

7B1.1

> 500:--: ‡a Ms.
> 500:--: ‡a Mss.
>
> 500:--: ‡a Ms. fragment.
> 500:--: ‡a Ms. fragments.
>
> 500:--: ‡a Ms. leaf.
> 500:--: ‡a Ms. leaves.
>
> 500:--: ‡a Ms. gathering.
> 500:--: ‡a Ms. gatherings.
>
> 500:--: ‡a Ms. component part.
>
> 500:--: ‡a Ms. codex.
>
> 500:--: ‡a Ms. composite codex.

500:--: ‡a Ms. document.
500:--: ‡a Ms. documents.

500:--: ‡a Ms. roll.
500:--: ‡a Ms. rolls.

7B1.2

520:--: ‡a Bible arranged in usual order with common set of prologues (see Ker, *Medieval Manuscripts in British Libraries*, I: 96–97).

520:--: ‡a Text of the Psalms with the Ordinary Gloss.

520:--: ‡a Text heavily annotated by a 16th cent. hand.

520:--: ‡a Collection of 132 documents (1580–1710) pertaining to property holdings of the Hale family in Hertfordshire, Cambridgeshire, Bedfordshire, Berkshire, and London. The manors of King's Walden (Herts.), White Waltham (Berks.), and Edworth (Beds.) are particularly well documented.

520:--: ‡a See printed catalog for full description.

7B2

546:--: ‡a Latin.

546:--: ‡a Old French.

546:--: ‡a Latin, with interlinear gloss in Old English.

546:--: ‡a Latin and Old French.

7B3

500:--: ‡a Title from rubric (fol. 2v).

500:--: ‡a Title from colophon (fol. 80r).

500:--: ‡a Title from spine, 17th cent.

500:--: ‡a Title added at head of text, 15th cent. (fol. 1r).

500:--: ‡a Title from printed catalog.

500:--: ‡a Title supplied by cataloger.

7B4

246:0-: ‡i Running title (passim): ‡a Consulta Basilii

246:0-: ‡i Title in prologue (fol. 1r): ‡a Regula Beati Basilii episcopi

246:0-: ‡i Title in explicit (fol. 93v): ‡a Consulta Basilii que dicuntur regula eiusdem

7B5.2

505:0-: ‡a Fol. 1r–4r: "[rubr.] Incipit regula sancti Augustini episcopi. [text] Ante omnia fratres karissimi diligatur Deus, deinde proximus … orans ut sibi debitum dimittatur et in temptationem non inducatur. [rubr.] Explicit regula sancti Augustini."

505:0-: ‡a 1. fol. 1r–33v: "[rubr.] Incipit prologus beati Iheronimi presbyteri in primum librum de vitis et doctrinis sanctorum patrum. [text] Benedictus Deus qui vult omnes homines salvos fieri … ; [fol. 2r: rubr.] Incipit liber primus de vitis et doctrinis sanctorum patrum editus ab Iheronimo. De sancto Iohanne abbate capitulum primum. [text] Primum igitur tamquam verum fundamentum nostri operis … et tanta nobis ostendit mirabilia ipsi gloria in secula seculorum. Amen. [rubr.] Explicit primus vitaspatrum." [PL 21:387–462].

505:8-: ‡a 2. fol. 33v–62v: "[rubr.] Incipit prologus in librum secundum. [text] Vere mundum quis dubitet meritis stare sanctorum … ; [fol. 34r: rubr.] Incipit liber secundus de verbis et doctrinis sanctorum patrum. [text] Quidam sanctorum seniorum patrum interrogantibus se monachis de causa abstinere dixit … quia interiori homini nostro sanitas inde crescit. [rubr.] Explicit liber secundus." [PL 73:739–810] …

505:0-: ‡a 1. fol. 1r: blank.

505:8-: ‡a 2. fol. 1v–149v: "[rubr.] Incipit prologus venerabilis Bede presbiteri. [text] Gloriosissimo regi Ceolvulfo Beda famulus christi et prespiter. Hystoriam gentis anglorum ecclesiasticam quam … ; [fol. 4r: rubr.] Britania oceani insula. [text] Cui quondam Albion nomen erat … letentur insule multe et confiteantur memorie sanctitatis eius. [rubr.] Explicit liber .v. hystorie gentis Anglorum."

7B5.3

505:0-: ‡a Fol. 1r–612v: Bible in usual order (see Ker, *Medieval Manuscripts in British Libraries* I:96–97), prologues cited precede text: General Prologue [Stegmüller 284]; Prologue to Pentateuch [Stegmüller 285], Genesis, Exodus, Leviticus, Numbers, Deuteronomy; Joshua [Stegmüller 311]; Judges; Ruth; 1 Kings [Stegmüller 323] …

505:0–: ‡a Fol. 1r–344v, Old Testament. fol. 1r–3r: "[rubr.] Incipit epistola beati Ieronimi ad Paulinum presbiterum de omnibus divinis historiis libris." [Stegmüller 284]; fol. 3r: "[rubr.] Alius prologus." [Stegmüller 285]; fol. 3r–18r: Genesis; fol. 18v–31r: "[rubr.] Incipit liber Exodi." fol. 31r–39v: "[rubr.] Incipit liber Levitici." fol. 39v–51v: "[rubr.] Incipit liber Numeri." fol. 51v–62r: "[rubr.] Incipit liber Deuteronomii." fol. 62r+v: "[rubr.] Incipit prologus super librum Iosue." [Stegmüller 311]; fol. 62v–70r: "[rubr.] Incipit liber Iosue." fol. 70r–77v: "[rubr.] Hic incipit liber Iudicum." fol. 77v–78v: "[rubr.] Incipit liber Ruth." fol. 78v–79r: "[rubr.] Prologus." [in Reg.; Stegmüller 323]; fol. 79r–90r: "[rubr.] Incipit liber Regum primus." …

505:0–: ‡a 1. fol. 1r–12v: Calendar including the feasts of Herculanus (1 March), Zenobius (25 May, in red), Proculus (1 June), Laurentinus and Pergentinus (3 June), Alexander bishop (6 June), Romulus (6 July), Nabor and Felix (12 July), Anne (26 July), "Sancte Marie ad nives" (5 August, in red), Transfiguration (6 August, in red), Donatus (7 August), Concordia (13 August), Potitus (6 September), Salvius (10 September), Reparata (8 October, in red), Cerbonius (10 October), "Fidriani" [sic, for Frediano; 18 November], Florentinus bishop (30 December).

505:8–: ‡a 2. fol. 13r–111v: "[rubr.] Incipit offitium beate Marie virginis secundum consuetudinem romane curie."

505:8–: ‡a 3. fol. 112r–176v: Office of the Dead. fol. 177r+v ruled but blank.

505:8–: ‡a 4. fol. 178r–214r: Long Hours of the Cross. fol. 214v–215v ruled but blank.

505:8–: ‡a 5. fol. 216r–221r: Short Hours of the Cross. fol. 221v ruled but blank.

505:8–: ‡a 6. fol. 222r–239r: Penitential psalms.

505:8–: ‡a 7. fol. 239r–252r: Litany, including Zenobius. fol. 252v ruled but blank.

505:0–: ‡a 1. fol. 1r–6v: Sarum calendar in purple, red, and black, partly graded. Added obit of "Thomas Minstrecha miles," A.D. 1452, at 19 Nov.

505:8–: ‡a 2. fol. 7v–12v: Table of statutes and chapters.

505:8–: ‡a 3. fol. 13r: "[rubr.] Magna carta. [text] Edwardus dei gracia … T. Edwardo filio nostro apud Westm' xi [sic] die Octobris anno regni nostri xxv. Dat' per manum nostram apud Westm' xxviii die Marcii anno regni nostri xxix [sic]." [SR I:116].

505:8–: ‡a 4. fol. 20r: "[rubr.] Incipit sentencia eiusdem carta." [SR I:6].

505:8–: ‡a 5. fol. 21r: "[rubr.] Incipit carta de foresta." Confirmation of 12 [sic] Oct. 1297 [SR I:120].

505:8–: ‡a 6. fol. 24v: "[rubr.] Incipiunt provisiones de Merton." [SR I:1].

505:8–: ‡a 7. fol. 28v: "[rubr.] Incipit Statutum de Marlebergh." [SR I:19].

505:8–: ‡a 8. fol. 39r: "[rubr.] Incipit Statutum Westm' primi." In French. [SR I:26].

505:8–: ‡a 9. fol. 58r: "[rubr.] Incipit Statutum Gloucestr'." In French. [SR I:45].

505:8–: ‡a 10. fol. 63r: "[rubr.] Incipiunt explanaciones eiusdem." [SR I:50] …

7B5.4

505:0–: ‡a 1. fol. 1r–93v: Regula / Saint Basil, Bishop of Caesarea.

505:8–: ‡a 2. fol. 94r–160v: De institutis coenobiorum et de octo principalium vitiorum remediis libri XII / John Cassian.

505:8–: ‡a 3. fol. 161r–211v: Regula / Saint Benedict, Abbot of Monte Cassino.

505:8–: ‡a 4. fol. 211v–259v: Liber de praecepto et dispensatione / Saint Bernard of Clairvaux.

505:8–: ‡a 5. fol. 259v–268v: Praeceptum / Saint Augustine, Bishop of Hippo.

7B6

246:1–: ‡i Secundo folio: ‡a Desiderium flagrans

246:1–: ‡i Secundo folio [text]: ‡a Tempus predicte

246:1–: ‡i Secundo folio [commentary]: ‡a Cum accessissent

246:1–: ‡i Secundo folio [calendar, fol. 3r]: ‡a KL Marcius

246:1–: ‡i Secundo folio [text, fol. 9r]: ‡a In exitu hii

7B7.1

500:––: ‡a Collation: Parchment, fol. ii (paper: Briquet, Armoiries, 1656) + 66 + ii (paper: Briquet, Armoiries, 1656) ; 1–10⁶11⁸(-2, 6) ; quires signed i-xi.

500:––: ‡a Collation: Parchment, fol. iii (modern paper) + ii (medieval parchment, ruled but blank) + 248 + ii (medieval parchment, ruled but blank) + iii (modern paper) ; 1² 2⁸(-1, fol. 1, with loss of text) 3–10¹⁰ 11¹⁰(-4, fol. 92, without loss of text) 12–26¹⁰ 27² ; horizontal catchwords in red ink frames.

7B8

500:––: ‡a Layout: Written in 25 long lines; frame-ruled.

500:––: ‡a Layout: Written in 2 columns of 35 lines, above line; ruled.

500:––: ‡a Layout: Written in 2 columns of 30 lines; frame-ruled in ink with double inner and outer vertical bounding lines; prickings in outer margin.

500:––: ‡a Layout: Written in 2 columns, below top line, 20 lines for text, 40 lines for commentary. Text ruled in lead on alternate lines in inner column; continuous commentary ruled in dry point in outer column.

7B9

500:––: ‡a Script: Written in a chancery hand.

500:––: ‡a Script: Written in medium grade, gothic book script (littera minuscula gothica textualis libraria).

500:––: ‡a Script: Written in insular phase II half-uncial, with interlinear Old English gloss in Anglo-Saxon pointed minuscule.

500:––: ‡a Script: Written by 3 scribes in an early Anglicana book script (Anglicana formata). Scribe 1, fol. 1r–75v; scribe 2, fol. 75v–140r; scribe 3, fol. 140r–210v.

7B10

500:––: ‡a Decoration: Illuminated initials and ten miniatures.

500:––: ‡a Decoration: Historiated initials at head of each chapter.

500:––: ‡a Decoration: Pen-flourished initials throughout.

500:––: ‡a Decoration: Primary (5- to 6-line) and secondary (2- to 3-line) pen-flourished initials throughout.

500:––: ‡a Decoration: Historiated initials (8-line) at head of each chapter (fols. 1r, 25r, 61v, 80r).

500:––: ‡a Decoration 1: Calendar illustrations: fol. ir, Jan. (Janus Feasting / Aquarius); fol. ivr, Feb. (Unshod man by fire holding boot / Pisces) …

500:––: ‡a Decoration 2: Historiated initials, major Psalm divisions: fol. 7r, Ps. I, B (King David playing harp in upper compartment / David beheading Goliath in lower compartment); fol. 49r, Ps. 38, D (David kneeling and pointing to eyes before enthroned Christ) …

500:––: ‡a Decoration 3: Decorated illuminated initials: (a) 4-line gold "KL" in calendar on bi-partite rose and blue ground patterned in white; (b) 2-line Psalm initials, other than major divisions, alternately in rose and blue, simply patterned in white, on rectangular grounds of opposite color, in-filled with foliate- or dragon-rinceau, some incorporating head of human or beast, bird, quadruped, or hybrid, with bird or quadruped perched atop some initials.

500:––: ‡a Decoration 4: Flourished initials: (a) Psalm versal, set off: gold and blue alternately, flourished in blue and red respectively; Dominical letters "A" in calendar: blue, flourished in red.

500:––: ‡a Decoration 5: Line-fillers: Red, gold, and blue stylized foliate or geometric patterns, regularly alternating with panels containing animate motifs in orange, copperous green, blue, rose, light brown, favorite motifs include dragons (usually holding round object in jaws), mitered or tonsured hybrids, static or running quadrupeds, fish.

500:--: ‡a Decoration 6: Marginal pen sprays, in red and blue descending diagonally across lower margins; on versos issuing at left from extension of Psalm-initial, versal, or independent head of human or beast; on rectos, typically issuing from tail or head at right end of nearest line-filler.

7B11

500:--: ‡a Music: Contains musical notation.

500:--: ‡a Music: Contains alphabetic notation.

500:--: ‡a Music: Contains neumatic notation (Hufnagel).

500:--: ‡a Music: Contains staff notation (4 line).

7B12

500:--: ‡a Binding: Modern.

500:--: ‡a Binding: 20th cent. Parchment wrapper.

500:--: ‡a Binding: 17th cent., early. Three-quarter calf, gold tooled.

500:--: ‡a Binding: 15th cent. Original sewing on five slit, tawed straps laced into wooden boards. Endband cords laid in grooves. Covered with white, tawed skin, blind-tooled with a St. Andrew's cross within panel borders. The covering leather is sewn around the endbands, from spine to edges, with a backstitch. Traces of round bosses, probably brass, and of two straps and pin fastenings, the pins on the upper board.

7B13

500:--: ‡a Accompanying materials: With 1 seal (green, oval, 2.1 x 3.2 cm.), pendant on a tag, bearing a fleur-de-lys and the legend: "S JOHANNIS LE ABE."

500:--: ‡a Accompanying materials: With 1 seal (red, 2.5 cm. diam.), applied, bearing a stag.

500:--: ‡a Accompanying materials: With 3 tags for seals (missing)

7B14

500:--: ‡a Origin: Written in northern France, probably first half of the 13th-cent. See notes on script.

500:--: ‡a Origin: Written in Paris in 1370 by Iohannes de Papeleu. "Anno Domini millesimo trecentesimo septimo decimo, hoc opus transcriptum est a Iohanne de Papeleu, clerico Parisius commoranti in vico Scriptorum, quem velit servare Deus qui est retributor omnium bonorum in secula seculorum. Amen." (fol. 506).

500:--: ‡a Origin: Produced in Paris in 1318 by Thomas de Maubeuge for Pierre Honnorez du Neuf Chastel. "[rubr.] Ci commencent les chroniques des roys de France ... lesquelles Pierres Honnorez du Nuef Chastel en Normandie fist escrire et ordener en la maniere que elles sont, selonc l'ordenance des croniques de Saint Denis, a mestre Thomas de Maubeuge, demorant en rue nueve Nostre Dame de Paris, l'an de grace Nostre Seigneur MCCCXVIII." (fol. 2r).

7B15

561:--: ‡a Inscription and date on fol. i recto: "En Vsu et scriptura 1573." Inscription inside front cover, in hand of 16th-cent. (visible under ultraviolet light): "Dono possideo | G Selb DX [?]". Signature of "Jac. Roch" with date "20 Aprilis 1793" on fol. 1r; later inscription "Bought of Mr. Roche of Cork," probably identifiable as James Roche, 1770–1853; DNB, v. 17, p. 69. Belonged to Sir Thomas Phillipps (no. 3899; stamp and notation inside front cover; tag on spine). From the library of George Dunn of Woolley Hall near Maidenhead (1865–1912, booklabel and inscription "dbl/ G D. | May 1903" inside front cover; his sale at Sotheby's, 2 Feb. 1914, no. 1573). Two unidentified entries from sales catalog pasted inside front cover and on first flyleaf. Belonged to Henry Fletcher.

7B16

541:--: ‡a Gift of Mrs. Henry Fletcher, 1953.

541:--: ‡a Purchased from H.P. Kraus, 1949, April 23.

7B17

500:--: ‡a Former shelfmark: Bury St. Edmunds, MS S.155.

500:--: ‡a Former shelfmark: Phillipps MS 21975.

500:--: ‡a Related shelfmark: Oxford, Bodleian Library, MS. Hatton 115.

7B18

500:--: ‡a Byname: Ellesmere Chaucer.

500:--: ‡a Byname: Medici Vergil.

500:--: ‡a Byname: Parker Chronicles and Laws.

500:--: ‡a Byname: Vienna Dioscurides.

500:--: ‡a Byname: Manesse Codex, Manessische Handschrift, Heidelberger Liederhandschrift, …

7B19

500:--: ‡a Shelfmark: Oxford, Bodleian Library, MS. Douce 217.

500:--: ‡a Shelfmark: Paris, Bibliothèque nationale de France, ms. fr. 10135.

500:--: ‡a Shelfmark: Vienna, Österreichische Nationalbibliothek, Hs. 2564.

500:--: ‡a Shelfmark: New York, Pierpont Morgan Library. MS M.1.

500:--: ‡a Shelfmark: Munich, Bayerische Staatsbibliothek, Cod. Gall. 4.

7B20

510:4-: ‡a Schutzner, S. Med. and Ren. bks. in LC, ‡c I, 6

510:4-: ‡a De Ricci, ‡c p. 180, no. 1

510:4-: ‡a Fay & Bond, ‡c p. 117, no. 1

7B21

581:--: ‡a PL, 103, cols. 485-554.

581:--: ‡a Hunter Blair, P. Moore Bede. Early English mss in facsimile, 9

581:--: ‡a Hamburger, J.F. Rothschild Canticles.

7B22

530:--: ‡a Also available in microfilm: ‡c for use in library only.

530:--: ‡a Also available in CD ROM (illuminations only).

530:--: ‡a Also available in digital format: ‡c accessible through library website.

530:--: ‡a Partial transcription of text (paper: 20th cent.): ‡c for use in library only.

7B23

533:--: ‡a Microfilm. ‡b Vatican City : ‡c Biblioteca Apostolica Vaticana, ‡d 1958. ‡e 1 microfilm reel ; 35 mm.

533:−−: ‡a Microfiche. ‡b Binghamton, N.Y. : ‡c Medieval & Renaissance Texts & Studies, ‡d 1994–. ‡e 1 microfiche; ‡f (Anglo-Saxon Manuscripts in Microfiche Facsimile, ASM 1.1 ; Medieval & Renaissance Texts & Studies, 136–137).

7B24

506:−−: ‡a Access limited: Use of reproduction preferred.

506:−−: ‡a Access restricted: Apply to curator of manuscripts.

506:−−: ‡a Available for consultation in East Reading Room only.

7B25

540:−−: ‡a Apply for permission to publish.

540:−−: ‡a Reproduction limited by copyright.

540:−−: ‡a Digital images protected by copyright.

7B26

Original
535:1–: ‡a Biblioteca Apostolica Vaticana; ‡c Vatican City ‡g vc

Reproduction
535:2–: ‡3 Microfilm ‡a Knights of Columbus Vatican Film Library, Pius XII Memorial Library, Saint Louis University; ‡b 3650 Lindell Boulevard, St. Louis, MO 63108; ‡c USA; ‡d 314-977-3090 ‡gmou

7B27

583:−−: ‡z Item cataloged in hand by [*name of cataloger*], [*date*]

583:−−: ‡z Item cataloged from microform reproduction by [*name of cataloger*], [*date*]

583:−−: ‡z Item cataloged from existing description: [*reference to published or unpublished description*]

583:−−: ‡z Item cataloged in hand by [*name of cataloger*], [*date*]; revised by [*name of cataloger*], [*date*]; decoration description provided by [*name of cataloger*], [*date*] …

APPENDIX A: ADDED ENTRY ACCESS

A3.1.1

752:--: ‡a France ‡c Normandy ‡d Rouen.

752:--: ‡a Belgium ‡c Flanders ‡d Ghent.

752:--: ‡a Italy ‡d Rome.

752:--: ‡a Spain ‡c Catalonia.

A3.1.2

100:1-: ‡a Chaucer, Geoffrey, ‡d d. 1400.
240:10: ‡a Canterbury tales
500:--: ‡a Byname: Ellesmere Chaucer.
500:--: ‡a Shelfmark: San Marino, CA, Henry E. Huntington Library, MS EL 26 C 9.
730:0-: ‡a Ellesmere Chaucer.

130:0-: ‡a Codex Nuttall.
500:--: ‡a Byname: Codex Nuttall, Codex Zouche, Codex Zouche-Nuttall.
500:--: ‡a Shelfmark: London, British Library, MS Additional 39671.

110:2-: ‡a Catholic Church.
240:10: ‡a Book of hours (Ms. De Brailes)
500:--: ‡a Byname: William de Brailes hours, De Brailes hours.
500:--: ‡a Shelfmark: London, British Library, MS Additional 49999.
730:0-: ‡a De Brailes hours.

110:2-: ‡a Catholic Church.
240:10: ‡a Book of hours (Ms. Honnold Library. Crispin 20)
500:--: ‡a Shelfmark: Claremont, CA, Honnold Library, MS Crispin 20.
710:2-: ‡a Honnold Library for the Associated Colleges. ‡k Manuscript. ‡n Crispin 20.

110:2-: ‡a Catholic Church.
240:10: ‡a Psalter (Ms. Blanche of Castile)
500:--: ‡a Byname: St. Louis and Blanche of Castile psalter, Blanche of Castile psalter, Royal psalter.
500:--: ‡a Shelfmark: Paris, Bibliothèque de l'Arsenal, ms. 1186.
730:0-: ‡a Blanche of Castile psalter.

130:0-: ‡a Haggadah (Ms. Rylands)

500:––: ‡a Byname: Rylands haggadah, Rylands Spanish haggadah, Ryland Sephardi haggadah.
500:––: ‡a Shelfmark: Manchester, John Rylands Library, MS Heb. 6.
730:0–: ‡a Rylands haggadah.

130:0–: ‡a Bible. ‡p N.T. ‡p Revelation. ‡l Latin. ‡s Trinity apocalypse.
500:––: ‡a Byname: Trinity apocalypse, Trinity College apocalypse.
500:––: ‡a Shelfmark: Cambridge, Trinity College, MS 950 (R.16.2).
730:0–: ‡a Trinity apocalypse.

710:2–: ‡a Henry E. Huntington Library and Art Gallery. ‡k Manuscript. ‡n BA 29.

710:2–: ‡a British Library. ‡k Manuscript. ‡n Cotton Otho A. XII.

710:2–: ‡a Biblioteca apostolica vaticana. ‡k Manuscript. ‡n Vat. lat. 679.

710:2–: ‡a Corpus Christi College (University of Cambridge). ‡b Library. ‡k Manuscript. ‡n 173, fol. 1r–56r.

A3.2.1

See 7B6

A3.2.2

700:1–: ‡a Du Neuf Chastel, Pierre Honnorez, ‡e former owner.

700:1–: ‡a Roche, James, ‡e former owner.

700:1–: ‡a Phillipps, Thomas, ‡c Sir, ‡d 1792–1872, ‡e former owner.

700:1–: ‡a Dunn, George, ‡e former owner.

700:1–: ‡a Fletcher, Henry, ‡e former owner.

APPENDIX D:
MARC 21 CATALOGING
RECORD EXAMPLES

The following examples present summary and detailed descriptions for two types of manuscripts. The first set of examples (I) illustrates catalog records for a manuscript containing two literary works, first given summary description (Ia) and then given detailed description (Ib) with both host-item and analytic constituent part records. The second example (II) illustrates the catalog record for a legal document given detailed description.

I. LITERARY WORKS

San Marino, CA, Henry E. Huntington Library, MS HM 34807

Source of Information:
Dutschke, *Huntington Library*, II:704–705 (some modifications made for the purpose of illustration)

Ia. Summary Catalog Record (no analysis of constituent works)

OCLC

Type:	t	ELvl:		Srce:		Audn:		Ctrl:		Lang:	lat
BLvl:	m	Form:		Conf:		Biog:		MRec:		Ctry:	enk
		Cont:		GPub:		LitF:	0	Index:	0		
Desc:	a	Ills:		Fest:		DtSt:	q	Dates:	1250, 1299		

```
040:––:  ‡e amremm
100:0–:  ‡a Petrus, ‡c Comestor, ‡d 12th cent.
240:10:  ‡a Historia scholastica
245:10:  ‡a Hystoria evangelium. ‡b Hystoria actuum apostolorum … [etc.].
260:––:  ‡a [England, ‡c between 1250 and 1299]
300:––:  ‡a 278 leaves : ‡b parchment, ill. ; ‡c 174 x 126 (134 x 95) mm. bound to 184 x 136 mm.
500:––:  ‡a Ms. codex.
```

520:--: ‡a Old and New and Testament Biblical histories, with genealogical tables from the Old Testament added. See printed catalog for full description.

546:--: ‡a Latin.

500:--: ‡a Collective title from closing and opening rubrics (fol. 246r).

505:0-: ‡a 1. fol. ir: Old Testament genealogies schematically displayed in an English hand of the end of the 13th-cent. or early 14th-cent.

505:8-: ‡a 2. ff.1r–246r: Historia scholastica / Peter Comestor.

505:8-: ‡a 3. fol. 246r–278v: Historia actuum apostolorum / Peter of Poitiers.

500:--: ‡a Layout: Written in 2 columns of 40 lines; frame-ruled.

500:--: ‡a Script: Written in an English book hand.

500:--: ‡a Decoration: Pen-flourished initials in red and blue.

500:--: ‡a Binding: Modern, 19th cent.

500:--: ‡a Origin: Written in England in the second half of the 13th cent.

500:--: ‡a Shelfmark: San Marino, CA, Henry E. Huntington Library, MS HM 34807.

510:4-: ‡a Dutschke, C.W. Med. and Ren. mss. in the Huntington Library, ‡c II:704-705

510:4-: ‡a Preston, J. "Medieval Manuscripts at the Huntington: Supplement to De Ricci's Census," Chronica, ‡c vol. 21, 1977, p. 7

583:--: ‡z Cataloged from existing description: Dutschke, C.W. Med. and Ren. mss. in the Huntington Library, ‡c II:704-705.

630:00: ‡a Bible. ‡p N.T. ‡p Gospels. ‡l Latin ‡v Commentaries ‡v Early works to 1800.

630:00: ‡a Bible. ‡p N.T. ‡p Acts. ‡l Latin ‡v Commentaries ‡v Early works to 1800.

630:00: ‡a Bible. ‡p N.T. ‡p Gospels. ‡l Latin ‡v Paraphrases ‡v Early works to 1800.

630:00: ‡a Bible. ‡p N.T. ‡p Acts. ‡l Latin ‡v Paraphrases ‡v Early works to 1800.

630:00: ‡a Bible. ‡p N.T. ‡p Gospels. ‡l Latin ‡x History of Biblical events ‡v Early works to 1800.

630:00: ‡a Bible. ‡p N.T. ‡p Acts. ‡l Latin ‡x History of Biblical events ‡v Early works to 1800.

650:-0: ‡a Manuscripts, Latin (Medieval and modern) ‡z California ‡z San Marino.

650:-0: ‡a Genealogy in the Bible ‡v Tables ‡v Early works to 1800.

655:-7: ‡a Gothic scripts. ‡2 aat

655:-7: ‡a Textura. ‡2 aat

700:02: ‡a Peter, ‡c of Poitiers, ‡d ca. 1130-1205. ‡t Historia actuum apostolorum.

710:2-: ‡a Henry E. Huntington Library and Art Gallery. ‡k Manuscript. ‡n HM 34807.

752:--: ‡a England.

Ib. Detailed Catalog Record

Host Item Record:

OCLC

Type:	t	ELvl:		Srce:		Audn:		Ctrl:		Lang:	lat
BLvl:	m	Form:		Conf:		Biog:		MRec:		Ctry:	enk
		Cont:		GPub:		LitF:	0	Index: 0			
Desc:	a	Ills:		Fest:		DtSt:	q	Dates: 1250, 1299			

040:––: ‡e amremm

100:1–: ‡a Petrus, ‡c Comestor, ‡d 12th cent.

240:10: ‡a Historia scholastica

245:10: ‡a Hystoria evangelium. ‡b Hystoria actuum apostolorum … [etc.].

246:1–: ‡i Secundo folio: ‡a dicunt eum

260:––: ‡a [England, ‡c between 1250 and 1299]

300:––: ‡a 278 leaves : ‡b parchment, ill. ; ‡c 174 x 126 (134 x 95) mm. bound to 184 x 136 mm.

500:––: ‡a Ms. codex.

520:––: ‡a Old and New and Testament Biblical histories, with genealogical tables from the Old Testament added.

546:––: ‡a Latin.

500:––: ‡a Collective title from closing and opening rubrics (fol. 246r).

505:0–: ‡a 1. fol. ir: Old Testament genealogies schematically displayed in an English hand of the end of the 13th-cent. or early 14th-cent.

505:8–: ‡a 2. ff.1r–246r: Historia scholastica / Peter Comestor.

505:8–: ‡a 3. fol. 246r–278v: Historia Actuum Apostolorum / Peter of Poitiers.

500:––: ‡a Collation: Parchment, fol. i (modern paper) + 278 + i (modern paper); 1–11^{12} 12^{8}(–5, 6, 7) 13–17^{12} 18^{6} 19–24^{12} 25^{4}(–4); quires 10–15 signed G–M apparently on each (?) leaf in blue; catchword on fol. 137v, in the inner corner, cropped.

500:––: ‡a Layout: Written in 2 columns of 40 lines, some columns divided into 2 narrower columns (e.g., on fol. 98v, 100); frame-ruled in lead; double bounding lines.

500:––: ‡a Script: Written in an English book hand.

500:––: ‡a Decoration: Opening initial, 6-line, parted red and blue with filigree infilling around 4 blue rosettes, with red and blue cascade and flourishing to frame the inner and upper margins. Blue initials, 2-line, with red and blue cascade or red flourishing; initials within the text touched in red; paragraph marks alternating in red and blue. Running headlines in red and blue.

500:––: ‡a Binding: Modern, 19th cent., in faded green calf.

500:––: ‡a Origin: Written in England in the second half of the 13th cent.

561:––: ‡a On fol. i verso, written in pale red ink in a mid-16th or 17th cent. legal anglicana script, probably in explanation of the name "Radulphus" on fol. 278v: "This books appears to have been examined by Radulph de Baldock, Deane of Saint Paule 1297." Ralph de Baldock, bishop of London, 1306-13, and chancellor of England, 1307, owned a number of books: Emden, BRUO, 2147–49, prints the list of the 37 books found in Baldock's study (June 1313) and of the 126 "libri scholastici" which Baldock bequeathed to St. Paul's in London, included at item 12 is "Historie scholastice cum aliis scriptis"; however, this book does not appear in St. Paul's 1458 catalog, printed by W. Dugdale, History of St. Paul's Cathedral in London (London 1716), 60–70. Stegmüller (7091–7092) notes a similar case of the name of Radulphus, whether possessor or author, added to the end of a Biblical commentary in a manuscript once at St. Paul's London. The manuscript belonged to Ebenezer Jacob, whose bookplate is on the front pastedown; later owned by John Broadley, with his bookplate on fol. i; his sales, Evans, 12 July 1832 and 19 June 1833 (these catalogs not available to us).

541:––: ‡a Acquired in 1971 from Lathrop C. Harper, Catalog 200 (Spring 1970), n. 9 with a plate of fol. 92r.

500:--: ‡a Shelfmark: San Marino, CA, Henry E. Huntington Library, MS HM 34807.

510:4-: ‡a Dutschke, C.W. Med. and Ren. mss. in the Huntington Library, ‡c II:704–705

510:4-: ‡a Preston, J. "Medieval Manuscripts at the Huntington: Supplement to De Ricci's Census," Chronica, ‡c vol. 21, 1977, p. 7

583:--: ‡z Cataloged from existing description: Dutschke, C.W. Med. and Ren. mss. in the Huntington Library, ‡c II:704–705.

650:-0: ‡a Manuscripts, Latin (Medieval and modern) ‡z California ‡z San Marino.

650:-0: ‡a Genealogy in the Bible ‡v Tables ‡v Early works to 1800.

655:-7: ‡a Bookplates (Provenance) ‡2 rbprov

655:-7: ‡a Gothic scripts. ‡2 aat

700:1-: ‡a Broadley, John, ‡e former owner.

700:1-: ‡a Jacob, Ebenezer, ‡e former owner.

700:1-: ‡a Baldock, Ralph de, ‡c Bishop of London, ‡d d. 1313, ‡e former owner.

710:2-: ‡a Henry E. Huntington Library and Art Gallery. ‡k Manuscript. ‡n HM 34807.

752:--: ‡a England.

774:00: ‡7 p0ta ‡a Petrus, Comestor, 12th cent. ‡s Historia scholastica. ‡t Hystoria evangelium, ‡d England, 1250–1299

774:00: ‡7 p0ta ‡a Peter of Poitiers, ca. 1130–1205. ‡s Historia actuum apostolorum. ‡t Hystoria actuum apostolorum, ‡d England, 1250–1299

Analyzed Constituent Work:

OCLC

Type: t	ELvl:	Srce:	Audn:	Ctrl:		Lang:	lat
BLvl: a	Form:	Conf:	Biog:	MRec:		Ctry:	enk
	Cont:	GPub:	LitF: 0	Index: 0			
Desc: a	Ills:	Fest:	DtSt: q	Dates: 1250, 1299			

040:--: ‡e amremm

100:0-: ‡a Petrus, ‡c Comestor, ‡d 12th cent.

240:10: ‡a Historia scholastica

245:10: ‡a Hystoria evangelium.

260:--: ‡a [England, ‡c between 1250 and 1299]

300:--: ‡a leaves 1r–246r: ‡b parchment ; ‡c 174 x 126 (134 x 95) mm. bound to 184 x 136 mm.

500:--: ‡a Ms. component part.

520:--: ‡a Old and New and Testament Biblical history by Peter Comestor.

546:--: ‡a Latin.

500:--: ‡a Title from closing rubric (fol. 246r).

505:0-: ‡a Fol. 1r–246r: "[prologue] Reverendo patri et domino Willelmo dei gratia Senonensi archiepiscopo … Causa suscepti laboris fuit instans petitio sociorum … ; [fol. 1r: text] Imperatorie maiestatis est in palatio ["tres" added in the margin, 14th cent.] habere mansiones … qui prius albula dicebatur, undecimus Silvius Agrippa. [fol. 137r–v, blank; text follows directly from fol. 136v to fol. 138r, beginning 4 Reg.:] Porro Ochosias filius Achab regnare cepit in Samaria … de Iohanne filio Symonis prosequentes. [fol. 197v, in the margin, note of missing text, 15th cent., being the inset "additiones"; fol. 198r, blank; fol. 198v, beginning the New Testament:] Mortuo symone qui ultimus v filiorum Mathathie Asamonei dux … et nota differentiam, translatus Enoch subvectus est Helyas, ascendit Ihesus propria sui virtute. [rubr.] Explicit Hystoria Evangelium."

500:--: ‡a Shelfmark: San Marino, CA, Henry E. Huntington Library, MS HM 34807.

510:4-: ‡a Dutschke, C.W. Med. and Ren. mss. in the Huntington Library, ‡c II:704–705

510:4-: ‡a Preston, J. "Medieval Manuscripts at the Huntington: Supplement to De Ricci's Census," Chronica, ‡c vol. 21, 1977, p. 7

581:--: ‡a PL 198: cols. 1053–1524C, 1525B–1644.

583:--: ‡z Cataloged from existing description: Dutschke, C.W. Med. and Ren. mss. in the Huntington Library, ‡c II:704–705.

630:00: ‡a Bible. ‡p O.T. ‡p Gospels. ‡l Latin ‡v Commentaries ‡v Early works to 1800.

630:00: ‡a Bible. ‡p O.T. ‡p Gospels. ‡l Latin ‡v Paraphrases ‡v Early works to 1800.

630:00: ‡a Bible. ‡p O.T. ‡p Gospels. ‡l Latin ‡x History of Biblical events ‡v Early works to 1800.

650:-0: ‡a Manuscripts, Latin (Medieval and modern) ‡z California ‡z San Marino.

710:2-: ‡a Henry E. Huntington Library and Art Gallery. ‡k Manuscript. ‡n HM 34807, fol. 1r–246r.

752:--: ‡a England.

773:0-: ‡7nntm ‡t Hystoria evangelium. Hystoria actuum apostolorum, ‡d England, 1250–1299

Analyzed Constituent Work:

OCLC

Type:	t	ELvl:		Srce:		Audn:		Ctrl:			Lang:	lat
BLvl:	a	Form:		Conf:		Biog:		MRec:			Ctry:	enk
		Cont:		GPub:		LitF:	0	Index:	0			
Desc:	a	Ills:		Fest:		DtSt:	q	Dates:	1250, 1299			

040:--: ‡e amremm

100:0-: ‡a Peter, ‡c of Poitiers, ‡d ca. 1130–1205.

240:10: ‡a Historia actuum apostolorum

245:10: ‡a Hystoria actuum apostolorum.

260:--: ‡a [England, ‡c between 1250 and 1299]

300:--: ‡a leaves 246r–278v : ‡b parchment ; ‡c 174 x 126 (134 x 95) mm. bound to 184 x 136 mm.

500:--: ‡a Ms. component part.

520:--: ‡a New Testament Biblical history by Peter of Poitiers.

546:--: ‡a Latin.

500:--: ‡a Title from opening rubric (fol. 246r).

505:0-: ‡a Fol. 246r–278v: "[rubr.] Incipiunt capitula Hystorie Actuum Apostolorum. [text] Anno nonodecimo imperii Tyberii Cesaris adhuc procuratore Iudee Pilato … et in loco honorabili scilicet in cathacumbis. [rubr.] Explicit Hystoria Actum Apostolorum Radulph[i?]."

500:‒‒: ‡a Shelfmark: San Marino, CA, Henry E. Huntington Library, MS HM 34807.

510:4‒: ‡a Dutschke, C.W. Med. and Ren. mss. in the Huntington Library, ‡c II:704–705.

510:4‒: ‡a Preston, J. "Medieval Manuscripts at the Huntington: Supplement to De Ricci's Census," Chronica, ‡c vol. 21, 1977, p. 7

581:‒‒: ‡a PL 198: cols. 1645–1722.

581:‒‒: ‡a Stegmüller 6565.

581:‒‒: ‡a Stegmüller 6785.

583:‒‒: ‡z Cataloged from existing description: Dutschke, C.W. Med. and Ren. mss. in the Huntington Library, ‡c II:704–705.

630:00: ‡a Bible. ‡p N.T. ‡p Gospels. ‡l Latin ‡v Commentaries ‡v Early works to 1800.

630:00: ‡a Bible. ‡p N.T. ‡p Acts. ‡l Latin ‡v Commentaries ‡v Early works to 1800.

630:00: ‡a Bible. ‡p N.T. ‡p Acts. ‡l Latin ‡v Paraphrases ‡v Early works to 1800.

630:00: ‡a Bible. ‡p N.T. ‡p Acts. ‡l Latin ‡x History of Biblical events ‡v Early works to 1800.

650:‒0: ‡a Manuscripts, Latin (Medieval and modern) ‡z California ‡z San Marino.

710:2‒: ‡a Henry E. Huntington Library and Art Gallery. ‡k Manuscript. ‡n HM 34807, fol. 246r–278v.

752:‒‒: ‡a England.

773:0‒: ‡7nntm ‡t Hystoria evangelium. Hystoria actuum apostolorum, ‡d England, 1250–1299

II. Legal Document—Detailed Catalog Record

Washington, D.C., Folger Shakespeare Library, MS X.d.92.

Sources of information:

> Jean F. Preston and Laetitia Yeandle, *English Handwriting, 1400–1650: An Introductory Manual* (Binghamton, N.Y.: Medieval & Renaissance Texts & Studies, 1992), no. 8.
> *Catalog of Manuscripts of the Folger Shakespeare Library*, 3 vols. (New York: G.K. Hall, 1971), II:103.

OCLC

Type:	t	ELvl:		Srce:		Audn:		Ctrl:			Lang:	eng
BLvl:	m	Form:		Conf:		Biog:		MRec:			Ctry:	enk
		Cont:		GPub:		LitF:	0	Index:	0			
Desc:	a	Ills:		Fest:		DtSt:	s	Dates:	1458			

040:‒‒: ‡e amremm

110:10: ‡a England. ‡b Sovereign (1483–1485 : Richard III)

245:10: ‡a [Warrant, 1485 May 28, to William Catesby to fell and carry wood in the parish of Nuthurst (Sussex)].

300:‒‒: ‡a 1 sheet : ‡b parchment ; ‡c 159 x 213 mm. + ‡e 1 seal.

500:‒‒: ‡a Ms. document.

520:‒‒: ‡a Warrant under the signet to fell and carry all the wood previously granted to William Catesby "… as is growing w[i]t[h]in the Grove called the peche conteynyng sex acres in the p[ar]isshe of Nuthurst being now in the holding of oon Davy Tussingh[a]m. whiche he[re]tofor[e] belonged vnto o[u]r Rebell s[ir] william Noreys ..." With the king's sign manual at top: "R[icardus] R[ex]."

546:--: ‡a English.

500:--: ‡a Title supplied by cataloger.

500:--: ‡a Script: Written in a careful secretary hand.

500:--: ‡a Accompanying materials: With 1 seal (fragmentary), applied, signet of Richard III (red, 27 mm.), in a rush ring.

500:--: ‡a Origin: "Yeuen vndre oure signet at our[e] Castell of Kenelworth' the xxviijti Day of May The secunde yere of oure Reigne."

541:--: ‡a Purchased from Maggs Bros., 1924 September, cat. 454, no. 2115.

500:--: ‡a Shelfmark: Washington, D.C., Folger Shakespeare Library, MS. X.d.92.

510:4-: ‡a Cat. of mss. of the Folger Shakespeare Library, ‡c II, p. 103

510:4-: ‡a De Ricci, ‡c p. 396, no. 1298.1

581:--: ‡a Preston & Yeandle. English handwriting, no. 8.

583:--: ‡z Item cataloged from existing descriptions.

600:00: ‡a Richard ‡b III, ‡c King of England, ‡d 1452–1485 ‡v Autographs.

600:00: ‡a Richard ‡b III, ‡c King of England, ‡d 1452–1485.

650:-0: ‡a Manuscripts, Medieval ‡z Washington (D.C.)

650:-0: ‡a Manuscripts, English ‡z Washington (D.C.)

651:-0: ‡a England ‡v Charters, grants, privileges.

651:-0: ‡a Sussex (England) ‡v Charters, grants, privileges.

651:-0: ‡a Nuthurst Parish (England) ‡v Charters, grants, privileges.

655:-7: ‡a Deeds ‡z England ‡z Sussex. ‡2 lcsh

655:-7: ‡a Deeds ‡z England ‡z Nuthurst Parish. ‡2 lcsh

655:-7: ‡a Warrants (Law) ‡z Great Britain. ‡2 lcsh

655:-7: ‡a Seals (Numismatics) ‡z Great Britain. ‡2 lcsh

655:-7: ‡a Signet seals ‡z Great Britain. ‡2 local

655:-7: ‡a Rush rings. ‡2 local

655:-7: ‡a Documentary scripts ‡z Great Britain. ‡2 aat

655:-7: ‡a Secretary scripts ‡z Great Britain. ‡2 local

700:0-: ‡a Richard ‡b III, ‡c King of England, ‡d 1452–1485.

700:1-: ‡a Catesby, William, ‡d d. 1485.

700:1-: ‡a Tussingham, David.

700:1-: ‡a Norreys, William, ‡c Sir.

710:2-: ‡a Folger Shakespeare Library. ‡k Manuscript. ‡n X.d.92.

752:--: ‡a England ‡b Sussex ‡c Nuthurst Parish.

752:--: ‡a England ‡b Warwickshire ‡d Kenilworth.

APPENDIX E: CONCORDANCE BETWEEN RULES IN AACR2R, DCRB, AND APPM

The following concordance provides analogues and parallel and comparative references between rules in *AMREMM* and those in *AACR2R*, *DCRB*, and *APPM*. In some cases there is direct one-to-one correspondence between these cataloging guides. The references provided here should be interpreted rather as sources (some adopted directly, others modified, and others rejected) that were considered in constructing the rules for *AMREMM*.

AMREMM	AACR2R	DCRB	APPM
0. GENERAL RULES			
0A	2.0A1, 2.12A, 4.0A1	0A	1.0A
0B1	1.0A1, 1.0A2, 1.0H1, 1.0H2, 1.1A2, 2.0B1, 2.13A, 4.0B1	0C1, 0C2, 0C3	1.0B
0B1.1			
0B2	2.0B2, 4.0B2	0D	1.0B2
0C	1.0C1, 2.0C	0E	1.0C
0D	1.0D, 1.0D1, 1.0D2, 1.0D3, 2.0D	0B1, Appendix D	1.0D, 1.0D1, 1.0D2
0E	1.0E1	0F	1.0E
0F			
0F1			
0F2.1		0H, Appendix B	
0F2.2	2.14E1, LCRI 1.0E	0H, Appendix B	
0F3	1.0G1	0H	1.0G

AMREMM	AACR2R	DCRB	APPM
0F4			
0F5	1.0F1	0G	1.0F
0F6	1.0F1	0G	1.0F
0F7			
0F8	1.0C1	0J1, 0J2	1.0C

1. TITLE AND STATEMENT OF RESPONSIBILITY AREA

AMREMM	AACR2R	DCRB	APPM
1A1	1.1A1, 2.1A1, 4.1A1	1A1	1A1
1A2.1	1.1A2	1A2	
1A2.2	1.1A2, 2.14C	1A2, 1B4	
1A2.3	1.0H1	0C2	
1B1.1	1.1B1, 1.1B2, 2.1B1, 4.1B1	1B1, 1B2, 1B3	1.1B1
1B1.2			
1B1.3			
1B1.4	1.1G1, 4.1G1	1E1, 1E2	1.1G
1B1.5	1.1G2, 1.1G3, 1.1G4, 4.1G1	1E1, 1E2	1.1G
1B1.6	1.1B7, 2.14A, 4.1B2	1B5	1.1B2
1B2.1	1.4F1, 1.4F2, 1.4F9, 4.1B2, 22.17A	4D2	1.1B2,1.1B4, 1.1B5, 1.1E1
1B2.2	4.1B2		1.1B2, 1.1B4, 1.1B5, 1.1E1
1B2.3	4.1B2		1.1B2,1.1B4, 1.1B5, 1.1E1
1C	1.1C, 2.1C, 4.1C		1.1C
1D1	1.1D3	1C	1.1D1
1D2	1.1D4	1C	1.1D1
1E1	1.1E1, 1.1E2, 1.1E3, 1.1E4, 1.1E5, 2.1E1, 2.14D, 4.1E	1D1, 1D2, 1D3, 1D4, 1D5, 1D6	1.1E1
1E2	1.1E6		1.1E1
1F1	1.1F1, 1.1F2, 2.1F1, 4.1F1, 4.1F3	1G1	1.1F
1F2	1.1F1	1G1	1.1F
1F3	1.1F3	1G3	
1F4	1.1F6	1G6	
1F5	1.1F7	1G7, 1G8	
1F6	21.4C	7C6	

AMREMM	AACR2R	DCRB	APPM
2. EDITION/VERSION AREA			
2A1	1.2B4, 2.2B3, 4.2A1	2.B5	1.2A1, 1.2B3
2A2	1.2A1, 2.1A1, 4.2A2	2A1	1.2A2
2A3	1.2A2		
2B1	1.1B2, 2.2B3, 2.15B, 4.2A1	2B6	1.2B3
2B2	1.2B1, 2.2B1, 2.15A, 4.2B1	2B1	1.2B1
2C	1.2C1, 1.2D1, 2.2C1, 2.2D1, 4.2C1	2C1	1.2C1
3. MATERIAL SPECIFIC DETAILS AREA			
3A	1.3A, 2.3A, 4.3A	3	1.3
4. PLACE AND DATE OF PRODUCTION AREA			
4A1			1.4
4A2	1.4A1, 2.4A1, 4.4A1	4A1	1.4
4A3	1.4A2, 1.5A3, 1.11, LCRI 1.11	4A2	
4B1	1.4B1, 1.4C8, 1.4D9, 1.4F9		
4B2	1.4B4		
4B3	1.4B6, 1.4F2	4B9	
4C1	1.4C1, 2.4C1, 2.16B	4B1, 4B10, 4B11	
4C2	1.4C6	4.B12	
4C3	1.4C5, 1.4D5, 1.4F8	4B6, 4B7	
4D1	1.4F1, 2.4F1, 2.16F	4D1, 4D2, 4D3	
4D2	1.4F7, 2.16G	4D5, 4D6	
4D3	1.4F8	4D7, 4D8	
5. PHYSICAL DESCRIPTION AREA			
5A1	1.5A1, 2.5A1, 4.5A1	5A1	1.5A1
5A2	1.5A2	5A2	
5A3	1.5A3, LCRI 1.11		
5B1	1.5B1, 2.5B1, 2.17A1	5B1	1.5B1, 1.5B2
5B2	2.5B2, 2.5B3, 2.5B4, 2.5B5, 2.5B6, 2.5B7, 2.5B8, 2.5B11, 2.5B12, 2.5B13, 2.5B14, 2.5B15, 2.5B16, 2.17A1, 4.5B1	5B1, 5B2, 5B3, 5B4, 5B5, 5B6, 5B7, 5B8, 5B10, 5B11, 5B12, 5B14, 5B15	1.5B1, 1.5B2

AMREMM	AACR2R	DCRB	APPM
5B3	2.5B6	5B6	
5B4	1.5B3, 2.5B17, 2.5B18, 2.5B19, 2.5B20, 2.5B21, 4.5B2	5B16, 5B17, 5B18, 5B19, 5B20, 5B21	1.5B1, 1.5B2
5B5	4.5B2		1.5B1, 1.5B2
5C1	1.5C1, 4.5C1	5C1, 5C2, 5C3,	1.5C1
5C2	1.5C1, 2.5C1, 2.5C2, 2.5C3, 2.5C4, 2.5C5, 2.5C6, 2.5C7, 2.17B1, 4.5C2	5C4, 5C5, 5C6, 5C7	1.5C1
5D1	1.5D1, 2.5D1, 2.17C1, 4.5D1	5D1	1.5D2
5D2			
5D3	2.5D4, 2.17C1, 4.5D2	5D5	1.5D2
5D4			
5E1	1.5E1, 2.5E1	5E1	

6. SERIES AREA

AMREMM	AACR2R	DCRB	APPM
6A	4.6A	6	1.6

7. NOTE AREA

AMREMM	AACR2R	DCRB	APPM
7A1	1.7A1, 2.7A1, 2.18A, 4.7A1	7B1	1.7A1
7A2	1.7A2, 2.7A2, 4.7A2	7B2	
7A3	1.7A3	7B3	
7A4		7A	
7A4.1			
7A4.2			
7B	1.7B, 2.7B, 2.18A, 4.7B	7C	1.7B
7B1	1.7B1, 2.7B1, 4.7B1	7C1	1.7B2
7B1.1	1.7B1, 2.7B1, 4.7B1	7C1	1.7B2
7B1.2	1.7B1, 2.7B1, 4.7B1	7C1	1.7B2
7B2	1.7B2, 2.7B2, 4.7B2	7C2	1.7B8
7B3	1.7B3, 2.7B3, 2.18B1, 4.7B3	7C3	1.7B17
7B4	1.7B4, 2.7B4, 4.7B4, 4.7B5	7C4, 7C5, 7C6	1.7B17
7B5.1.1	1.7B18, 2.7B18, 4.7B18	7C16	1.7B2, 1.7B7
7B5.1.2	1.7B18, 2.7B18, 4.7B18	7C16	1.7B2, 1.7B7
7B5.2	1.7B18, 2.7B18, 4.7B18	7C16	1.7B2, 1.7B7
7B5.3	1.7B18, 2.7B18, 4.7B18	7C16	1.7B2, 1.7B7

AMREMM	AACR2R	DCRB	APPM
7B5.4	1.7B18, 2.7B18, 4.7B18	7C16	1.7B2, 1.7B7
7B6	4.7B23		1.7B17
7B7	2.18D1, 4.7B23	7C9	1.7B17
7B7.1	2.18D1, 4.7B23	7C9	1.7B17
7B7.2	2.18D1, 4.7B23	7C9	1.7B17
7B7.3	2.18D1, 4.7B23	7C9	1.7B17
7B8	1.7B10, 2.7B10, 2.18E1, 4.5B1	7C10	1.7B17
7B9	4.7B23		1.7B17
7B10	1.7B10, 2.7B10, 2.18F1, 4.7B23	7C18	1.7B17
7B11			
7B12	1.7B10, 2.7B10, 2.18F1, 4.7B23	7C18	1.7B17
7B13	1.7B11, 2.7B11, 4.7B11	7C11	
7B14	4.7B8		
7B15	4.7B7	7C18	1.7B9
7B16	4.7B7		1.7B10
7B17			
7B18			
7B19			
7B20	1.7B15, 2.18C1, 4.7B15	7C14	1.7B14
7B21	2.18C1, 4.7B9	7C14	1.7B16
7B22	1.7B16, 2.7B16		1.7B4
7B23			1.7B5
7B24	4.7B14		1.7B11
7B25	4.7B14		1.7B12
7B26			1.7B6
7B27			

APPENDIX A. ADDED ENTRY ACCESS

A1	21.29		2.2
A2	21.30		2.3
A2.1	21.30A1		2.3A
A2.2	21.30M1	Appendix A 1E1–1E2	
A2.3	21.30J	Appendix A General provision, 0G, 0J2, 1B1, 1B3, 1E1–1E2, 7C4–7C5	2.3G
A3			
A3.1			

AMREMM	AACR2R	DCRB	APPM
A3.1.1			
A3.1.2			
A3.2			
A3.2.1			
A3.2.2			

APPENDIX B. ANALYSIS

B1	13.6A		
B2			
B3			

APPENDIX F: MANUSCRIPT CATALOGING AND DESCRIPTION BIBLIOGRAPHY

Manuscript description and cataloging has traditionally been a highly individualized occupation, and, consequently, practices among catalogers vary depending upon personal style and circumstance. It is normally an individual cataloger who is responsible for producing the manuscript descriptions that make up his or her own catalog, and it is this individual who usually, therefore, also sets the descriptive criteria for cataloging. For instance, one cataloger may choose to focus upon decoration, another upon script, and neither may use precisely the same formula to express the collation of a manuscript, though they both agree upon the arrangement of the leaves. National and institutional policies can also affect, or be reflected in, individual practice. Cataloging may be summary or highly detailed depending upon the scope of a given project. Indeed, the very heterogeneous nature of manuscripts themselves as a class of materials further promotes this diversity. Yet, for all the variety of practice to be found there is also a great degree of commonality, at least in the broad categories of description if not always in the manner in which their details are expressed.

Beyond establishing a certain desirable degree of uniformity, the present guidelines do not prescribe how the details of a description should be written or the nomenclature that should be used. They set out the broad descriptive categories of information that should be included in a description and how this information should be disposed in the catalog record. However, the manner in which a manuscript should be analyzed and described is rightly left to the discretion and expertise of the individual cataloger. These guidelines do not in themselves constitute a handbook to manuscript cataloging. For this reason, a bibliography is provided for those seeking further information on technical aspects of manuscript description and cataloging. It is divided into two sections: analysis, and cataloging and description. The first section attempts to set out standard works that are most immediately useful to the cataloger when analyzing the manuscript as an object, facilitating identification of typology and proper nomenclature for a given item or feature. It is highly selective and works have been chosen because they serve either as useful introductions to their respective subjects or as authoritative sources for reference, standard terminology, or bibliography. The result is a mix of works that are both introductory and highly specialized, but it is expected that the reader will be able to identify items through the references in these works that will satisfy further inquiry. The second section provides an introduction to cataloging theory and practice, and lays out the sources for what may be understood as the Anglo-American tradition of manuscript cataloging.

I. Analysis

Introductory

- James Douglas Farquhar, "The Manuscript as a Book," in Sandra Hindman and James Douglas Farquhar, *Pen to Press: Illustrated Manuscripts and Printed Books in the First Century of Printing* (College Park, Md.: Art Department, University of Maryland, 1977), 11–99.
- Robert G. Calkins, *Illuminated Books of the Middle Ages* (Ithaca, N.Y.: Cornell University Press, 1983).
- Otto Pächt, *Book Illumination in the Middle Ages: An Introduction*, trans. Kay Davenport (London: Harvey Miller, 1986).
- Otto Mazal, *Lehrbuch der Handschriftenkunde*, Elemente des Buch- und Bibliothekswesens, 10 (Wiesbaden: Ludwig Reichert Verlag, 1986).
- Barbara A. Shailor, *The Medieval Book: Illustrated from the Beinecke Rare Book and Manuscript Library*, Medieval Academy Reprints for Teaching, 28 (Toronto: University of Toronto Press, 1991).
- L. D. Reynolds and N.G. Wilson, *Scribes and Scholars: A Guide to the Transmission of Greek and Latin Literature*, 3rd ed. (Oxford: Clarendon Press, 1991).
- Jonathan J.G. Alexander, *Medieval Illuminators and their Methods of Work* (New Haven: Yale University Press, 1992).
- Christopher de Hamel, *Scribes and Illuminators* (London: British Library; Toronto: University of Toronto Press, 1992).
- Christopher de Hamel, *A History of Illuminated Manuscripts*, 2nd ed. (London: Phaidon, 1994).
- Christopher de Hamel, *The British Library Guide to Manuscript Illumination: History and Techniques* (London: British Library; Toronto: University of Toronto Press, 2001).

Paleography

General

- Joachim Kirchner, *Scriptura gothica libraria a saeculo xii usque ad finem medii aevi* (Munich: Oldenbourg, 1966).
- E. A. Lowe, *Handwriting: Our Medieval Legacy* (Rome: Edizioni di storia e letteratura, 1969).
- S. Harrison Thomson, *Latin Bookhands of the Later Middle Ages, 1100–1500* (Cambridge: Cambridge University Press, 1969).
- Bernhard Bischoff, *Latin Palaeography: Antiquity and the Middle Ages*, trans. Dáibhí Ó Cróinín and David Ganz (Cambridge: Cambridge University Press, 1990). The standard paleographical manual in English.
- Michelle P. Brown, *A Guide to Western Historical Scripts from Antiquity to 1600* (Toronto: University of Toronto Press; London: British Library, 1990).
- Jacques Stiennon, *Paléographie du Moyen Âge*, 2nd ed. (Paris: Armand Colin, 1991).
- James J. John, "Latin Paleography," in *Medieval Studies: An Introduction*, ed. James M. Powell, 2nd ed. (Syracuse, N.Y.: Syracuse University Press, 1992): 3–81. An excellent introduction to the subject with extensive bibliography.
- Julian Brown, "Aspects of Palaeography," in *A Palaeographer's View: the Selected Writings of Julian Brown*, ed.

Janet Bately, Michelle P. Brown, and Jane Roberts (London: Harvey Miller, 1993), 47–91. A posthumous assemblage of earlier essays and a very good introduction to the discipline.

- M.B. Parkes, *Pause and Effect: An Introduction to the History of Punctuation in the West* (Berkeley: University of California Press, 1993).

Great Britain
- Charles Johnson and Hilary Jenkinson, *English Court Hand A.D. 1066 to 1500*, 2 vols. (Oxford: Clarendon Press, 1915).
- Hilary Jenkinson, *The Later Court Hands in England from the Fifteenth to the Seventeenth Century*, 2 vols. (Cambridge: Cambridge University Press, 1927; rpt. New York: Ungar, 1969).
- T.A.M. Bishop, *Scriptores regis: Facsimiles to Identify and Illustrate the Hands of Royal Scribes in Original Charters of Henry I, Stephen, and Henry II* (Oxford: Clarendon Press, 1961).
- L.C. Hector, *The Handwriting of English Documents*, 2nd ed. (London: Edward Arnold, 1966).
- Giles E. Dawson and Laetitia Kennedy-Skipton, *Elizabethan Handwriting, 1500–1650: A Manual*, rev. ed. (New York: Norton, 1968).
- M.B. Parkes, *English Cursive Book Hands, 1250–1500* (Oxford: Clarendon Press, 1969).
- T.A.M. Bishop, *English Caroline Minuscule* (Oxford: Clarendon Press, 1971).
- N.R. Ker, *English Manuscripts in the Century after the Norman Conquest* (Oxford: Clarendon Press, 1960).
- Anthony G. Petti, *English Literary Hands from Chaucer to Dryden* (Cambridge, Mass.: Harvard University Press, 1977).
- Jean F. Preston and Laetitia Yeandle, *English Handwriting, 1400–1650: An Introductory Manual* (Binghamton, N.Y.: Medieval & Renaissance Texts & Studies, 1992).

France
- Maurice Prou, *Manuel de paléographie latine et française*, 4th ed. (Paris: Picard, 1924).
- Emmanuel Poulle, *Paléographie des écritures cursives en France du XVᵉ au XVIIᵉ siècle* (Geneva: Droz, 1966).
- Gabriel Audisio and Isabelle Bonnot-Rambaud, *Lire le français d'hier: Manuel de paléographie moderne, XVᵉ-XVIIIᵉ siècle* (Paris: Armand Colin, 1991).

Italy/Renaissance
- B.L. Ullman, *The Origin and Development of Humanistic Script* (Rome: Edizione di Storia e Letteratura, 1960).
- Alfred Fairbank and Berthold Wolpe, *Renaissance Handwriting: An Anthology of Italic Scripts* (London: Faber and Faber, 1960).
- James Wardrop, *The Script of Humanism: Some Aspects of Humanist Script, 1460–1560* (Oxford: Clarendon Press, 1963).
- Vincenzo Federici, *La scrittura delle cancellarie Italiane dal secoli XII al XVII* (Rome: Pompeo Sansaini, 1934).
- E.A. Loew, *The Beneventan Script: A History of the South Italian Minuscule*, ed. Virginia Brown, 2nd ed., 2 vols., Sussidi Eruditi, 33–34 (Rome: Edizioni di Storia e Letteratura, 1980).

Spain
- Jesús Muñoz y Rivero, *Manual de paleografía diplomatica española de los siglos XII al XVII: Método téorico-práctico para aprender a leer los documentos españoles de los siglos XII al XVII*, 2nd ed. (Madrid: Vidua de Hernando, 1889; rpt. Madrid: Atlas, 1970).

- Jesús Muñoz y Rivero, *Paleografía visigoda: Método teórico-práctico para aprender a leer los codices y documentos españoles de los siglos V al XII* (Madrid: Daniel Jorro, 1919).
- Zacarias García Villada, *Paleografía española: Precedida de una introducción sobre la paleografía latina* (Madrid: Revista de filologia española, 1923; rpt. Barcelona: Ediciones El Albir, 1974.)
- Antonio Cristino Floriano Cumbreño, *Curso general de paleografía y diplomatica españolas*, 2 vols. (Oviedo: Imprenta la Cruz, 1946).
- Augustín Millares Carlo and José Manuel Ruiz Asencio, *Tratado de paleografía española*, 3rd ed., 3 vols. (Madrid: Espasa-Calpe, 1983).

Codicology

- L. M. J. Delaissé, "Towards a History of the Medieval Book," *Codicologica 1: Théories et principes*, Litterae textuales (Leiden: E.J. Brill, 1976), 75–83.
- Jean Vezin, "La Réalisation matérielle des manuscrits latins pendant le haut Moyen Âge," *Codicologica, 2: Eléments pour une codicologie comparée*, Litterae textuales (Leiden: E.J. Brill, 1978), 15–51.
- Albert Derolez, *Codicologie des manuscrits en écriture humanistique sur parchemin*, 2 vols., Bibliologia: Elementa ad librorum studia pertinentia, 5–6 (Turnhout: Brepols, 1984).
- Jacques Lemaire, *Introduction à la codicologie*, Publications de l'Institut d'études médiévales, Université catholique de Louvain, textes, études, congrès, 9 (Louvain-la-Neuve: Université catholique de Louvain, 1989).
- Albert Derolez, "La Codicologie et les études médiévales," in *Bilan et perspectives des études médiévales en Europe: Actes du premier Congrès européen d'études médiévales (Spoleto, 27–29 mai 1993)*, ed. Jacqueline Hamesse, Fédération internationale des instituts d'études médiévales, textes et études du Moyen Âge, 3 (Louvain-la-Neuve: Fédération internationale des instituts d'études médiévales, 1995), 371–86.

Diplomatics

- Arthur Giry, *Manuel de diplomatique* (Paris: Hachette, 1894; rpt. Hildesheim: G. Olms, 1972).
- Alain de Boüard, *Manuel de diplomatique française et pontificale*, 2 vols. (Paris: Picard, 1929-52)
- Harry Breslau, *Handbuch der Urkundenlehre für Deutschland und Italien*, 3rd ed., 3 vols. (Berlin: W. de Gruyter, 1958–68).
- Georges Tessier, *Diplomatique royale française* (Paris: Picard, 1962).
- Hilary Jenkinson, *Guide to Seals in the Public Records Office*, 2nd ed. (London: H.M.S.O., 1968).
- Pierre Chaplais, *English Royal Documents: King John – Henry VI, 1199–1461* (Oxford: Clarendon Press, 1971).
- Michel Pastoreau, *Les Sceaux*, Typologie des sources du Moyen Âge occidental, 36 (Turnout: Brepols, 1981).
- Leonard E. Boyle, "Diplomatics," in *Medieval Studies: An Introduction*, ed. James M. Powell, 2nd ed. (Syracuse: Syracuse University Press, 1992), 82–113. A very good introduction to the subject with extensive bibliography.
- Olivier Guyotjeannin, Jacques Pycke, and Benoît-Michel Tock, *Diplomatique médiévale*, L'Atelier du médiéviste, 2 (Turnhout: Brepols, 1993). Comprehensive overview of the subject with extensive bibliography.
- P. D. A. Harvey and Andrew McGuinness, *A Guide to British Medieval Seals* (Toronto: University of Toronto Press, 1996).

Binding

- E. Ph. Goldschmidt, *Gothic & Renaissance Bookbindings*, 2nd ed., 2 vols. (London: Vellekoop, 1928; rpt. Nieuwkoop: B. de Graaf; Amsterdam: N. Israel, 1967).
- Berthe Van Regemorter, "Évolution de la technique de la reliure du viiie au xiie siècle," *Scriptorium* 2 (1948): 275–85, translated as "Evolution of Binding Technique from the VIIIth to the XIIth Century," in *Binding Structures in the Middle Ages: A Selection of Studies*, trans. Jane Greenfield, Studia Bibliothecae Wittockianae, 3 (Brussels: Bibliotheca Wittockiana; London: Maggs Bros., 1992), 23–41.
- *The History of Bookbinding 525–1950 A.D.: An Exhibition held at the Baltimore Museum of Art November 12, 1957 to January 12, 1958* (Baltimore: Walters Art Gallery, 1957).
- Graham Pollard, "Describing Medieval Bookbindings," in *Medieval Learning and Literature: Essays Presented to Richard William Hunt*, ed. J.J.G. Alexander and M. T. Gibson (Oxford: Clarendon Press, 1976), 50–65.
- Léon Gilissen, *La Reliure occidentale antérieure à 1400*, Bibliologia: Elementa ad librorum studia pertinentia, 1 (Turnhout: Brepols, 1983).
- Carlo Federici, *La Legatura medievale*, 2 vols., Addenda: Studi sulla conoscenza, la conservazione e il restauro del materiale librario, 2 (Rome: Istituto centrale per la patologia del libro, 1993).
- Otto Mazal, *Einbandkunde: Die Geschichte des Bucheinbandes*, Elemente des Buch- und Bibliothekswesens, 16 (Wiesbaden: Ludwig Reichert Verlag, 1997).
- Jean-Louis Alexandre and Claire Maître, *Catalogue des reliures médiévales conservées à la Bibliothèque municipale d'Autun, ainsi qu'à la Société d'Éduenne*, Reliures médiévales des bibliothèques de France, 1 (Turnhout: Brepols, 1997).
- J. A. Szirmai, *The Archaeology of Medieval Bookbinding* (Aldershot, Hants.: Ashgate, 1999). Includes an extensive bibliography.
- Jean-Louis Alexandre, Geneviève Grand, and Guy Lanoë, *Bibliothèque municipale de Vendôme*, Reliures médiévales des bibliothèques de France, 2 (Turnhout: Brepols, 2000).

Sacred scripture, liturgical, and devotional works:

- Victor Leroquais, *Les Sacramentaires et les missels manuscrits des bibliothèques publiques de France*, 3 vols. (Paris, 1924).
- Falconer Madan, "The Localization of Manuscripts," in *Essays in History Presented to Reginald Lane Poole*, ed. H.W.C. Davis (Oxford: Clarendon Press, 1927), 5–29.
- Victor Leroquais, *Les Livres d'heures manuscrits de la Bibliothèque nationale*, 2 vols. (Paris, 1927).
- Fernand Cabrol, *Les Livres de la liturgie latine* (Paris: Bloud & Gay, 1930), translated as *The Books of the Latin Liturgy* (St. Louis, Mo.: Herder, 1932).
- Paul Perdrizet, *Le Calendrier parisien à la fin du Moyen Age d'après le bréviaire et les livres d'heures* (Paris: Les Belles lettres, 1933).
- Victor Leroquais, *Les Bréviaires manuscrits de bibliothèques publiques de France*, 5 vols. (Paris, 1934).
- Victor Leroquais, *Les Pontificaux manuscrits des bibliothèques publiques de France*, 4 vols. (Paris, 1937).
- Victor Leroquais, *Les Psautiers: Manuscrits latins des bibliothèques publiques de France*, 2 vols. (Paris, 1940–41).
- John Plummer, *Liturgical Manuscripts for the Mass and the Divine Office* (New York: Pierpont Morgan Library, 1964).
- Guy Philippart, *Les Légendiers latins et autres manuscrits hagiographiques*, Typologie des sources au Moyen Âge occidental, 24–25 (Turnhout: Brepols, 1977).

- John P. Harthan, *The Book of Hours* (New York: Park Lane, 1977).
- Jaques Dubois, *Le Martyrologes du Moyen Âge latin*, Typologie des sources au Moyen Âge occidental, 26 (Turnhout: Brepols, 1978).
- F. P. Pickering, *The Calendar Pages of Medieval Service Books*, Reading Medieval Studies, 1 (Reading: Reading University Centre for Medieval Studies, 1980).
- Andrew Hughes, *Medieval Manuscripts for Mass and Office: A Guide to Their Organization and Terminology* (Toronto: University of Toronto Press, 1982).
- Christopher de Hamel, *Glossed Books of the Bible and the Origins of the Paris Book Trade* (Woodbridge, Suffolk: D. S. Brewer, 1984).
- Janet Backhouse, *Books of Hours* (London: British Library, 1985).
- Laura Light, *The Bible in the Twelfth Century: An Exhibition of Manuscripts at the Houghton Library* (Cambridge, Mass.: Harvard College Library, 1988).
- Michel Huglo, *Les Livres de chant liturgique*, Typologie des sources au Moyen Âge occidental, 52 (Turnhout: Brepols, 1988).
- Joseph Szövérffy, *Latin Hyms*, Typologie des sources au Moyen Âge occidental, 55 (Turnhout: Brepols, 1989).
- John Harper, *Forms and Orders of Western Liturgy from the Tenth to the Eighteenth Century: A Historical Introduction and Guide for Students and Musicians* (Oxford: Clarendon Press, 1991).
- Aimé Georges Martimort, *Les Lectures liturgiques et leurs livres*, Typologie des sources au Moyen Âge occidental, 64 (Turnhout: Brepols, 1992).
- Margaret T. Gibson, *The Bible in the Latin West*, The Medieval Book, 1 (Notre Dame, Ill.: University of Notre Dame Press, 1993).
- Knud Ottosen, *The Responsories and Versicles of the Latin Office of the Dead* (Aarhus: Aarhus University Press, 1993).
- Marcel Metzger, *Les Sacramentaires*, Typologie des sources au Moyen Âge occidental, 70 (Turnhout: Brepols, 1994).
- Eric Palazzo, *A History of Liturgical Books from the Beginning to the Thirteenth Century*, trans. Madeleine Beaumont (Collegeville, Minn.: Liturgical Press, 1998).
- Beverly Mayne Kienzle, ed., *The Sermon*, Typologie des sources au Moyen Âge occidental, 81–83 (Turnhout: Brepols, 2000).
- Jeanne E. Krochalis and E. Ann Matter, "Manuscripts of the Liturgy," in *The Liturgy of the Medieval Church*, ed. Thomas J. Heffernan and E. Ann Matter (Kalamazoo, Mich.: Western Michigan University, 2001), 433–72.
- Roger S. Wieck, *Time Sanctified: The Book of Hours in Medieval Art and Life*, 2nd ed. (New York: Braziller, 2001).
- Roger S. Wieck, "The Book of Hours," in *The Liturgy of the Medieval Church*, ed. Thomas J. Heffernan and E. Ann Matter (Kalamazoo, Mich.: Western Michigan University, 2001), 473–513.

Other types of manuscripts

- Peter Murray Jones, *Medieval Medicine in Illuminated Manuscripts*, rev. ed. (London: British Library, 1998).
- Leslie M. Smith, *Masters of the Sacred Page: Manuscripts of Theology in the Latin West to 1274*, The Medieval Book, 2 (Notre Dame, Ill.: University of Notre Dame Press, 2001).
- Susan L'Engle and Robert Gibbs, *Illuminating the Law: Medieval Legal Manuscripts in Cambridge Collections* (London: Harvey Miller, 2001).

Abbreviations

- Ludwig Traube, *Nomina sacra: Versuch einer Geschichte der christlichen Kurzung* (Munich: C.H. Beck, 1907).
- Charles Trice Martin, *The Record Interpreter*, 2nd ed. (London: Stevens, 1910; rpt. Hildesheim: G. Olms, 1969).
- W. M. Lindsay, *Notae Latinae: An Account of Abbreviations in Latin MSS. of the Early Minuscule Period (c. 700–850)* (Cambridge: Cambridge University Press, 1915; rpt. with a supplement by Doris Bains on Latin abbreviations in manuscripts 850–1050, Hildesheim: G. Olms, 1963).
- José López de Toro, *Abreviaturas hispanicas* (Madrid: Direccion General de Archivos y Bibliotecas, Junta Técnica de Archivos, Bibliotecas y Museos, 1957).
- Auguste Pelzer, *Abbréviations latines médiévales: Supplément au Dizionario di abbreviature latine ed italiane de Adriano Cappelli*, 2nd ed. (Louvain: Publications Universitaires; Paris: Béatrice-Nauwelaerts, 1966).
- Adriano Cappelli, *Lexicon abbreviaturarum: Dizionario di abbreviature latine ed italiane*, 6th ed. (Milan: Ulrico Hoepli, 1967).
- *The Elements of Abbreviation in Medieval Latin Paleography*, trans. David Heimann and Richard Kay, University of Kansas Publications, Library Series, 47 (Lawrence, Kans.: University of Kansas Libraries, 1982). Translation of Cappelli's introductory essay, "Brachigrafia medioevale," from the *Lexicon abbreviaturarum*.

Chronology

- Hermann Grotefend, *Zeitrechnung des deutschen Mittelalters und der Neuzeit*, 3 vols. (Hannover: Hahn, 1891–98; rpt. Aalen: Scientia, 1984)
- Adriano Cappelli, *Cronologia, cronografia e calendario perpetuo*, 2nd ed. (Milan: Hoepli, 1930).
- Reginald Lane Poole, *Medieval Reckonings of Time*, Helps for Students of History, 3 (London: Society for Promoting Christian Knowledge, 1935).
- V. Grumel, *La Chronologie* (Paris: Presses universitaires de France, 1958).
- Hermann Grotefend, *Taschenbuch der Zeitrechnung des deutschen Mittelalters und der Neuzeit*, 10. Aufl. (Hannover: Hahn, 1960).
- Eg. I. Strubbe, *De Chronologie van de Middeleeuwen en de Moderne Tijden in de Nederlanden* (Antwerp: Standaard-Boekhandel, 1960; rpt. Bruxelles: Palais de Académies, 1991).
- E. B. Fryde and F. M. Powicke, *Handbook of British Chronology*, 3rd ed., Royal Historical Society Guides and Handbooks, 2 (London: Royal Historical Society, 1986).
- R. Dean Ware, "Medieval Chronology," in *Medieval Studies: An Introduction*, ed. James M. Powell (Syracuse, N.Y.: Syracuse University Press, 1992), 252–77.
- C. R. Cheney, *A Handbook of Dates for Students of British History*, rev. ed., Royal Historical Society Guides and Handbooks, 4 (Cambridge: Cambridge University Press, 2000).

Nomenclature

- B. Bischoff, G. I. Lieftinck, and G. Battelli, *Nomenclature des écritures livresques du IXe au XVIe siècle (Colloque international de paléographie latine, Paris, 28–30 avril 1953)* (Paris: C.N.R.S., 1954).
- Lucia N. Valentine, *Ornament in Medieval Manuscripts: A Glossary* (London: Faber and Faber, 1965).
- M. B. Parkes, *English Cursive Book Hands, 1250–1500* (Oxford: Clarendon Press, 1969).
- J. P. Gumbert, "A Proposal for a Cartesian Nomenclature," in *Essays Presented to G.I. Lieftinck*, ed. J.P. Gumbert and M. J. M De Haan, 4 vols., Litterae textuales (Amsterdam: A. L. Van Gendt, 1972–76), IV:45–52.

- François Garnier, *Le Langage de l'image au Moyen Âge*, 2 vols. (Paris: Le Léopard d'Or, 1982).
- François Garnier, *Thesaurus iconographique: Système descriptif des représetations*, (Paris: Le Léopard d'Or, 1984).
- *Diplomatica et sigillographica: Travaux préliminaires de la Commission internationale de diplomatique et de la Commission internationale de sigillographie pour une normalisation internationale des éditions de documents et un vocabulaire international de la diplomatique et de la sigillographie.* Folia Caesaraugustana, 1. Publicación ... de la Institución Fernando el Católico, 964 (Zaragoza: Cátedra Zurita, 1984).
- Denis Muzerelle, *Vocabulaire codicologique: Répertoire méthodique des termes français relatifs aux manuscrits*, Rubricae, 1 (Paris: CEMI, 1985).
- G. I. Lieftinck and J. P. Gumbert, *Manuscrits datés conservés dans les Pays-Bas: Catalogue paléographique des manuscrits en écriture latine portant des indications de date, 2: Les Manuscrits d'origine Néerlandaise (XIVᵉ–XVIᵉ siècles)* (Leiden: E. J. Brill, 1988), 23–35.
- Olga Weijers, ed., *Vocabulaire du livre et de l'écriture au Moyen Âge: Actes de la table ronde, Paris, 24–26 septembre 1987*, Études sur le vocabulaire intellectuel du Moyen Âge, 2 (Turnhout: Brepols, 1989).
- Christine Jakobi, *Buchmalerei: Ihre Terminologie in der Kunstgeschichte* (Berlin: Dietrich Reimer, 1991).
- H.-P. Neuhauser, "Typologie und Terminologie liturgischer Bücher," *Bibliothek: Forschung und Praxis* 16 (1992): 45–65.
- T. J. Brown, "Names of Scripts: A Plea to all Medievalists," in *A Palaeographer's View: The Selected Writings of Julian Brown*, ed. Janet Bately, Michelle P. Brown, and Jane Roberts (London: Harvey Miller, 1993), 39–45.
- École des hautes études en sciences sociales, Paris. Groupe d'anthropologie historique de l'Occident médiéval, *Thésaurus des images médiévales pour la constitution de bases de données iconographiques* (Paris: Centre de recherches historiques; École des hautes études en sciences sociales, 1993).
- Michelle P. Brown, *Understanding Illuminated Manuscripts: A Guide to Technical Terms* (Malibu, Calif.: J. Paul Getty Museum; London: British Library, 1994).
- Pilar Ostos et al., *Vocabulario codicología*, Instrumenta bibliológica (Madrid: Arcos Libros, 1997).
- Marilena Maniaci, *Terminologia del libro manoscritto*, Addenda: Studi sulla conoscenza, la conservazione e il restauro del materiale librario, 3 (Rome: Istituto centrale per la patologia del libro, 1998).
- Jacques-Hubert Sautel, "Essai de terminologie de la mise en page des manuscrits à commentaire," *Gazette du livre médiéval* 35 (1999): 17–31.

II. Cataloging and description

Basic handbooks and practical manuals on how to catalog a manuscript—as opposed simply to concisely stated rules or instructions—are few, and this information tends to be dispersed. For explanation of the elements of a manuscript description, see:

- Otto Mazal, *Zur Praxis des Handschriftenbearbeiters*, Elemente des Buch- und Bibliothekswesens, 11 (Wiesbaden: Ludwig Reichert Verlag, 1987), translated as *The Keeper of Manuscripts*, Bibliologia: Elementa ad librorum studia pertinentia, 11 (Turnhout: Brepols, 1992), 16–24. Also includes an extensive bibliography of reference works commonly used in manuscript research.
- Armando Petrucci, *La descrizione del manoscritto: Storia, problemi, modelli*, Aggiornamenti, 45 (Rome: La Nuova Italia Scientifica, 1984). An excellent historical and comparative treatment of cataloging methodologies, as well as practical guidance.

Other useful introductory works are:
- Falconer Madan, *Books in Manuscript: A Short Introduction to their Study and Use*, 2ⁿᵈ ed., rev. (London: K. Paul,

Trench, Trubner & Co., 1920), 153–66.

- R. B. Haselden, *Scientific Aids for the Study of Manuscripts*, Supplement to the Bibliographical Society's transactions, 10 (Oxford: Oxford University Press, 1935), 1–26 (though much of the scientific information in this work is now outdated).
- E. Casamassima, "Note sul metodo della descrizione dei codici," *Rassegna degli Archivi di stato* 23 (1963): 181–205.
- L. M. J. Delaissé, James Marrow, and John de Wit, *Illuminated Manuscripts: The James A. de Rothschild Collection at Waddesdon Manor* (Fribourg: National Trust, 1977), 13–20. An excellent, concise discussion of the importance of paleographical, codicological, and decorative aspects in medieval book production and how these features contribute to a catalog description.
- Raymond Macken, "Bref vade-mecum pour la description sur place d'un manuscrit médiéval," *Bulletin de philosophie médiévale* 21 (1979): 86–97.
- Alexander R. Rumble, "Using Anglo-Saxon Manuscripts," in *Anglo-Saxon Manuscripts: Basic Readings*, ed. Mary P. Richards, Basic Readings in Anglo-Saxon England, 2 (New York: Garland, 1994), 3–24. Not directed to cataloging *per se*, but addresses those features of manuscripts (not limited to those of Anglo-Saxon origin) most important for researchers to take note of and to record.

The modern, Anglo-American tradition of manuscript cataloging generally follows the methods and standards developed by N.R. Ker for use in his own catalogs. See:

- N. R. Ker, *Medieval Manuscripts in British Libraries*, 4 vols. (Oxford: Clarendon Press, 1969–1992), I:vii-xiii. Outlines sixteen "points of method" for manuscript description.
- N. R. Ker, *Catalogue of Manuscripts containing Anglo-Saxon* (Oxford: Clarendon Press, 1957), xx–xxiii. Section on collation is reprinted in *Medieval Manuscripts in British Libraries*, III:vii.

Ker, in his turn, refined the methods and categories that had been elaborated earlier by M. R. James for use in his own catalogs. See:

- M. R. James, *A Descriptive Catalogue of the Manuscripts in the Fitzwilliam Museum* (Cambridge: Cambridge University Press, 1895), xix–xli. Discusses "Points to be Observed in the Description and Collation of Manuscripts, particularly Books of Hours."
- Richard W. Pfaff, "M. R. James on the Cataloguing of Manuscripts: A Draft Essay of 1906," *Scriptorium* 31 (1977): 103–18. A posthumously published brief essay on manuscript cataloging.

At the same time that M. R. James was cataloging manuscripts in Cambridge using a detailed, analytical method, Falconer Madan was implementing a summary method of cataloging for use in cataloging the manuscripts of the Bodleian Library in Oxford. See:

- Falconer Madan, *A Summary Catalogue of Western Manuscripts in the Bodleian Library at Oxford*, 7 vols. (Oxford: Clarendon Press, 1895–1953). Madan's approach is set out schematically in vol. 3, p. x, given historical and comparative background in vol. 1, pp. ix–lxxiv (esp. p. lxxiii), and provided with fuller explanation (with reference to Ker's method) in Albinia de la Mare, *Catalogue of the Collection of Medieval Manuscripts Bequeathed to the Bodleian Library, Oxford, by James P. R. Lyell* (Oxford: Clarendon Press, 1971), xxxi–xxxiii.

The method for expressing the collation of a manuscript used by Ker is widely employed, with more or less variation, within the Anglo-American cataloging tradition. This method differs significantly, however, from Continental methods. For a comparison of the two, see:

- Frank Bischoff, "Methoden der Lagenbeschreibung," *Scriptorium* 46 (1992): 3–27.

Many recent North-American manuscript catalogs explicitly acknowledge their debt to Ker. Their own statements of methodology and the examples provided by their entries offer valuable illustrations of the variety of ways in which Ker's method may be applied. Among these catalogs, see:

- Barbara A. Shailor, *Catalogue of Medieval and Renaissance Manuscripts in the Beinecke Rare Book and Manuscript Library, Yale University*, 3 vols., Medieval & Renaissance Texts & Studies, 34, 48, 100 (Binghamton, N.Y.: Medieval & Renaissance Texts & Studies, 1984-92), I:xviii–xxi.
- C. W. Dutschke and R. H. Rouse, *Medieval and Renaissance Manuscripts in the Claremont Libraries*, Medieval and Renaissance Manuscripts in California Libraries, 1, University of California Publications: Catalogs and Bibliographies, 3 (Berkeley: University of California Press, 1986), xv–xvii.
- C. W. Dutschke, *Guide to Medieval and Renaissance Manuscripts in the Huntington Library*, 2 vols. (San Marino, Calif.: Huntington Library, 1989), I:xv–xvii.
- Paul Saenger, *A Catalogue of the Pre-1500 Western Manuscript Books at the Newberry Library* (Chicago: University of Chicago Press, 1989), xiv–xvi.
- Mirella Ferrari, *Medieval and Renaissance Manuscripts at the University of California, Los Angeles*, ed. R. H. Rouse, Medieval and Renaissance Manuscripts in California Libraries, 2, University of California Publications: Catalogs and Bibliographies, 7 (Berkeley: University of California Press, 1991), xxv–xxvi.
- Laura Light, *Catalogue of Medieval and Renaissance Manuscripts in the Houghton Library, Harvard University*, Medieval & Renaissance Texts & Studies, 145 (Binghamton, N.Y.: Medieval & Renaissance Texts & Studies, 1995–), xvi–xviii.

For their particular attention to illumination, see:

- L. M. J. Delaissé, James Marrow, and John de Wit, *Illuminated Manuscripts: The James A. de Rothschild Collection at Waddesdon Manor* (Fribourg: National Trust, 1977).
- Lilian M. C. Randall, *Medieval and Renaissance Manuscripts in the Walters Art Gallery*, 3 vols. (Baltimore: Johns Hopkins University Press, 1988–97).

For its particular attention to textual details, see:

- Svato Schutzner, *Medieval and Renaissance Manuscript Books in the Library of Congress: A Descriptive Catalog*, 2 vols. (Washington, D.C.: Library of Congress, 1989–).

Among recent British catalogs in the tradition of Ker, see:

- R.A.B. Mynors, *Catalogue of the Manuscripts of Balliol College, Oxford* (Oxford: Clarendon Press, 1963).
- J. J.G. Alexander and A.C. de la Mare, *The Italian Manuscripts in the Library of Major J.R. Abbey* (New York: Praeger, 1969).
- Albinia de la Mare, *Catalogue of the Collection of Medieval Manuscripts Bequeathed to the Bodleian Library, Oxford, by James P.R. Lyell* (Oxford: Clarendon Press, 1971).
- M.B. Parkes, *The Medieval Manuscripts of Keble College, Oxford: A Descriptive Catalogue with Summary Descriptions of the Greek and Oriental Manuscripts* (London: Scholar Press, 1971).

- Andrew G. Watson, *Catalogue of Dated and Datable Manuscripts c.700–1600 in the Department of Manuscripts, the British Library*, 2 vols. (London: British Library, 1979).
- Andrew G. Watson, *Catalogue of Dated and Datable Manuscripts c.435–1600 in Oxford Libraries*, 2 vols. (Oxford: Clarendon Press, 1984).
- P.R. Robinson, *Catalogue of Dated and Datable Manuscripts c.737–1600 in Cambridge Libraries*, 2 vols. (Woodbridge, Suffolk: D. S. Brewer, 1988), I:1–12, 17–18. Discusses the nature of dating evidence in dated or datable manuscripts.
- R.M. Thomson, *Catalogue of the Manuscripts of Lincoln Cathedral Chapter Library* (Woodbridge, Suffolk: D. S. Brewer, 1989).
- R.A.B. Mynors and R. M. Thomson, *Catalogue of the Manuscripts of Hereford Cathedral Library* (Cambridge: D.S. Brewer, 1993). With a contribution on bindings by Michael Gullick.
- Andrew G. Watson, *A Descriptive Catalogue of the Medieval Manuscripts of All Souls College, Oxford* (Oxford: Oxford University Press, 1997), xx–xxiii.
- Andrew G. Watson, *A Descriptive Catalogue of the Medieval Manuscripts of Exeter College, Oxford* (Oxford: Oxford University Press, 2000).
- R.M. Thomson, *A Descriptive Catalogue of the Medieval Manuscripts in Worcester Cathedral Library* (Woodbridge, Suffolk: D. S. Brewer, 2001). With a contribution on bindings by Michael Gullick.

Manuscript fragments and individual leaves present their own special problems for identification, cataloging, and description. See:
- N.R. Ker, *Fragments of Medieval Manuscripts used as Pastedowns in Oxford Bindings, with a Survey of Oxford Binding, c. 1515–1620*, Oxford Bibliographical Society Publications, 5–8 (Oxford: Oxford Bibliographical Society, 1954), vii–xx.
- Rowan Watson, *Descriptive List of Fragments of Medieval Manuscripts in the University of London Library* (London: University of London Library, 1976), iii–xvi.
- Rowan Watson, "Medieval Manuscript Fragments," *Archives* 13 (1977): 61–73.
- Elisabeth Pellegrin, "Fragments et membra disiecta," *Codicologica 3: Essais typologiques*, Litterae textuales (Leiden: E. J. Brill, 1980), 70–95.
- William M. Voelkle and Roger S. Wieck, *The Bernard H. Breslauer Collection of Manuscript Illuminations* (New York: Pierpont Morgan Library, 1992).
- Robert G. Babcock, *Reconstructing a Medieval Library: Fragments from Lambach* (New Haven: Beinecke Rare Book & Manuscript Library, 1993).
- Roger S. Wieck, "Folia Fugitiva: The Pursuit of the Illuminated Manuscript Leaf," *Journal of the Walters Art Gallery* 54 (1996): 233–54.
- Christopher de Hamel, *Cutting Up Manuscripts for Pleasure and Profit* (Charlottesville, Va.: Book Arts Press, 1996).
- Sandra Hindman, Mirella Levi D'Ancona, Pia Palladino, and Maria Francesca Saffiotti, *The Robert Lehman Collection, IV: Illuminations* (Princeton, N.J.: Princeton University Press, 1997).
- Nicholas Pickwood, "The Use of Fragments of Medieval Manuscripts in the Construction and Covering of Bindings on Printed Books," in *Interpreting and Collecting Fragments of Medieval Books*, ed. Linda L. Brownrigg and Peggy Smith (Los Altos Hills, Calif.: Anderson-Lovelace/Red Gull Press, 2000), 1–20.
- Jan Brunius, "Medieval Manuscript Fragments in Sweden: A Catalogue Project," in *Interpreting and Collecting Fragments of Medieval Books*, ed. Linda L. Brownrigg and Peggy Smith (Los Altos Hills, Calif.: Anderson-Lovelace/Red Gull Press, 2000), 157–65.

- Jennifer M. Sheppard, "Medieval Binding Structures: Potential Evidence from Fragments," in *Interpreting and Collecting Fragments of Medieval Books*, ed. Linda L. Brownrigg and Peggy Smith (Los Altos Hills, Calif.: Anderson-Lovelace/Red Gull Press, 2000), 167–75.

For general considerations of cataloging theory and application not already cited above, see:

- Léopold Delisle, *Note sur le catalogue général des manuscrits des bibliothèques des départements* (Nogent-le-Rotrou: A. Gouverneur, 1873).
- Léopold Delisle, *Note sur les catalogues de la Bibliothèque nationale* (Lille: L. Danel, 1889).
- Andrew Clark, *The Cataloguing of MSS in the Bodleian Library: A Letter Addressed to Members of Congregation by the Outgoing Junior Proctor, 9 April 1890* (Oxford: Horace Hart, 1890).
- Franz Ehrle, "Zur Geschichte der Katalogisierung der Vatikana," *Historisches Jahrbuch* 11 (1890): 718–27.
- M. Ortiz, "Per la catalogazione dei manoscritti delle biblioteche governative italiane," *Accademie e biblioteche d'Italia* 5 (1931): 11–19.
- E.C. Richardson, *A Union World Catalog of Manuscript Books: Preliminary Studies in Method, 6: Studies in Method* (New York: H.W. Wilson, 1937). See the review by Auguste Pelzer, "Un Essai américain de catalogue sommaire de tous les manuscrits," *Revue d'histoire ecclésiastique* 32 (1936): 621–30; rpt. in *Études d'histoire littéraire sur la scholastique médiévale*, ed. Adrien Pattin and Émile van der Vyer, Philosophes médiévaux, 8 (Louvain: Publications universitaires; Paris: Béatrice-Nauwelaerts, 1964), 97–109.
- Dorothy May Norris, *A History of Cataloguing and Cataloguing Methods, 1100–1850* (London: Grafton, 1939).
- L. Denecke, "Über die Ausbildung einer Instruktion für das Verzeichnis der Handschriften im Deutschen Reich," *Zentralblatt für Bibliothekswesen* 57 (1940).
- Emil Wallner, "Inventarisierung und Katalogisierung von Handschriften," *Zentralblatt für Bibliothekswesen* 57 (1940): 52–60.
- Auguste Pelzer, "Osservazioni e reflessioni sui manoscritti e le biblioteche," in *Il libro e le biblioteche: Atti del primo congresso bibliologico francescano internazionale, 20–27 febbraio 1949*. 2 vols. (Rome: Pontificium Athenaeum Antonianum, 1950), I:399–412; translated as "Observations et réflexions sur les manuscrits et les bibliothèques," in *Études d'histoire littéraire sur la scholastique médiévale*, Philosophes médiévaux, 8 (Louvain: Publications Universitaires; Paris: Béatrice-Nauwelaerts, 1964), 21–34.
- Dorothy K. Coveney, "The Cataloguing of Literary Manuscripts," *The Journal of Documentation* 6 (1950): 125–39.
- W.J. Wilson, "Manuscript Cataloguing," *Traditio* 12 (1956): 457–555.
- Gilbert Ouy, "Pour une archivistique des manuscrits médiévaux," *Bulletin des bibliothèques de France* 3 (1958): 897–923.
- J. Porcher, "A propos des catalogues de manuscrits," *Bulletin des bibliothèques de France* 5 (1960): 79–82.
- G. Meyer, "Probleme der katalogisierung mittelalterlicher Handschriften," *Nachrichten der Vereinigung Schweizer Bibliotekare* 36 (1960): 1–9.
- Gilbert Ouy, "Projet d'un catalogue de manuscrits médiévaux adapté aux exigences de la recherche moderne," *Bulletin des bibliothèques de France* 6 (1961): 319–35.
- François Masai, "Le problème des catalogues de manuscrits médiévaux," *Bulletin des bibliothèques de France* 8 (1963): 1–10.
- G. Göller, "Methode des Katalogiesierens liturgischer Handschriften," *Mitteilungen der Arbeitsgemeinschaft für rheinische Musikgeschichte* 27 (1966): 90–91.

- M.L. Colker, "The Cataloguing of Medieval Manuscripts: A Review Article," *Mediaevalia et humanistica*, n.s., 2 (1971): 165–73.
- Albert Derolez, "Les nouvelles instructions pour le catalogue des manuscrits en Republique Fédérale allemande," *Scriptorium* 28 (1974): 299–300.
- M.C. Garand, "Le Catalogue des manuscrits datés en écriture Latine," *Codices manuscripti* 1 (1975): 97–103.
- Gilbert Ouy, "Comment rendre les manuscrits médiévaux accessibles aux chercheurs?" *Codicologica, 4: Essais méthodologiques*, Litterae textuales (Leiden: E. J. Brill, 1978), 9–58.
- Gerhardt Powitz, "Zur Textaufnahme in Handschriftenkatalogen," *Codicologica, 4: Essais méthodologiques*, Litterae textuales (Leiden: E. J. Brill, 1978), 59–66.
- Gilbert Ouy, "Pour une organisation internationale de documentation automatisée sur les manuscrits et les textes médiévaux," *Actas del V Congreso Internacional de Filosofia Medieval*, 2 vols. (Madrid: Editora Nacional, 1979), I:295–308.
- Paul Canart, "De la catalographie à l'histoire du livre: Vingt ans de recherche sur le manuscrits grecs," *Byzantion* 50 (1980): 563–616.
- A. Gruijs and P. Holager, "Plan for Computer-assisted Codicography of Medieval Manuscripts," *Quaerendo* 11 (1981): 95–127.
- Gerold Hayer, "Richtlinien oder Dogma? Ein Beitrag zur Diskussion über die Richtlinien für die Handschriftenbeschreibung in Österreich," in *Beiträge zur Überlieferung und Beschreibung deutscher Texte des Mittelalters (Referate der 8. Arbeitstagung österreichischer Handschriften-Bearbeiter vom 25.–28. 11. 1981 in Rief bei Salzburg)*, ed. Ingo Reiffenstein, Göppinger Arbeiten zur Germanistik, 402 (Göppingen: Kümmerle Verlag, 1983), 213–27.
- Felix Heinzer, "Les catalogues de manuscrits de la Deutsche Forschungsgemeinschaft," *Gazette du livre médiévale* 4 (1984): 6–8.
- Renate Schipke, "L'Inventaire central des manuscrits médiévaux conservés en République Démocratique Allemande," *Gazette du livre médiévale* 4 (1984): 8–10.
- Richard W. Clement, "Cataloging Medieval and Renaissance Manuscripts: A Review," *Library Quarterly* 55 (1985): 316–26.
- Joachim-Felix Leonhard, "Manuscripts and Humanist Research: Functions and Goals of Manuscript Cataloguing in the Federal Republic of Germany," *Libri* 37 (1987): 179–95.
- J. Corhouts, "A MARC Format for Medieval Codices," *Gazette du livre médiévale* 11 (1987): 13–17.
- Albert Derolez, "Catalogues codicologiques," *Gazette du livre médiévale* 12 (1988): 4–6.
- Hope Mayo, "Standards for Description, Indexing and Retrieval in Computerized Catalogs of Medieval Manuscripts," in *The Use of Computers in Cataloging Medieval and Renaissance Manuscripts: Papers from the International Workshop in Munich, 10–12 August 1989*, ed. Menso Folkerts and Andreas Kühne, Algorismus, 4 (München: Institut für Geschichte der Naturwissenschaften, 1990), 19–39.
- Lucien Reynhout, "Pour une typologie des catalogues de manuscrits médiévaux: Contribution à un inventaire collectif en Belgique," *Archives et bibliothèques de Belgique* 61 (1990): 5–37.
- Hope Mayo, "Medieval Manuscript Cataloging and the MARC Format," *Rare Books & Manuscripts Librarianship* 6, no. 1 (1990): 11–22.
- Mirella Ferrari, *Medieval and Renaissance Manuscripts at the University of California, Los Angeles*, ed. R.H. Rouse, Medieval and Renaissance Manuscripts in California Libraries, 2, University of California Publications: Catalogs and Bibliographies, 7 (Berkeley: University of California Press, 1991), xi–xvii.

- Hope Mayo, "MARC Cataloguing for Medieval Manuscripts: An Evaluation," in *Bibliographic Access to Medieval and Renaissance Manuscripts: A Survey of Computerized Data Bases and Information Services*, ed. Wesley M. Stevens (New York: Haworth Press, 1992), 93–152.

- Ambroggio M. Piazzoni, "Lavori e progetti per l'informatizzazione orientata allo studio dei manoscritti nella Biblioteca Apostolica Vaticana," in *Méthodologies informatiques et nouveaux horizons dans les recherches médiévales* (*Actes du Colloque international de Saint-Paul-de-Vence, 3–5 septembre 1990*), ed. Jacqueline Hamesse, Société internationale pour l'étude de la philosophie médiévale, rencontres de philosophie médiévale, 2 (Turnhout: Brepols, 1992): 159–76.

- Bernd Michael, "Handschriftenkatalogisierung in Deutschland: der Gesamtindex mittelalterlicher Handschriftenktaloge," *Gazette du livre médiévale* 21 (1992): 13–17.

- Elizabeth Yakel, "Pushing MARC-AMC to its Limits: The Vatican Archives Project," *American Archivist* 55 (1992): 192–201.

- Gilbert Ouy, "Vers des bases de données sur les manuscrits médiévaux: pour une code descriptif normalisé à plusieurs niveaux," *Gazette du livre médiévale* 20 (1992): 1–7.

- Richard W. Pfaff, "N.R. Ker and the Study of English Medieval Manuscripts," in *Anglo-Saxon Manuscripts: Basic Readings*, ed. Mary P. Richards, Basic Readings in Anglo-Saxon England, 2 (New York: Garland, 1994), 55–77.

- Peter van Minnen, "Introducing the Online Catalogue of the Duke Papyrus Collection," *Bulletin of the American Society of Papyrologists* 31 (1994): 159–70.

- Gerhardt Powitz, "Cataloguing Medieval Manuscripts: Work in Progress and Transition," in *Bilan et perspectives des études médiévales en Europe: Actes du permier Congrès européen d'ètudes médiévales* (*Spoleto, 27–29 mai 1993*), éd. Jacqueline Hamesse, Fédération internationale des instituts d'études médiévales, textes et études du Moyen Âge, 3 (Louvain-la-Neuve: Fédération internationale des instituts d'études médiévales, 1995), 387–97.

- Barbara A. Shailor, "A Cataloger's View," in *The Whole Book: Cultural Perspectives on the Medieval Miscellany*, ed. Stephen G. Nichols and Siegfried Wenzel (Ann Arbor, University of Michigan Press, 1996): 153–67.

- Rowan Watson, "Automation and the Medieval Manuscript: Out of MARC and into the Web," *Gazette du livre médiévale* 31 (1997): 41–46.

- Lou Burnard, Richard Gartner, and Peter Kidd, "The Cataloguing of Western Medieval Manuscripts in the Bodleian Library: A TEI Approach with an Appendix Describing a TEI-Conformant Manuscript Description," (URL: http://users.ox.ac.uk/~lou/wip/MS, August 1997).

- Eva Nilsson Nylander and Sever J. Voicu, "Queen Christina's Latin Manuscripts in the Vatican Library— A Cataloguing Project," in *Clavis memoriae: Ett seminarium om datoriserad katalogisering av handskriftsmaterial* (*Svenska institut I Rom, 22–26 april, 1996*), ed. Eva Nilsson Nylander, Kungl. Bilbioteket rapport, 23 (Stokholm: Kungl. Biblioteket, 1997), 82–92.

- Arno Mentzel-Reuters, "Literaturbericht Handschriftenkataloge," *Deutsches Archiv für Erforschung des Mittelalters* 54 (1998): 583–611.

- Gregory A. Pass, "Electrifying Research in Medieval and Renaissance Manuscripts," *Papers of the Bibliographical Society of America* 94 (2000): 507–30.

- Elizabeth O'Keefe, "Medieval Manuscripts on the Internet," *Journal of Religious & Theological Information* 3, no. 2 (2000): 9–47.

- Laurence S. Creider, "Accessing Medieval Religious Manuscripts on OCLC," *Journal of Religious & Theological Information* 3, no. 2 (2000): 49–63.

- Guilia Ammannati, "La Catalogazione del manoscritto: Alcune riflessioni," *Scritura e civiltà* 24 (2000): 375–85.

For discussions of a wider range of issues in manuscript cataloging, the proceedings of a number of conferences and collected studies devoted to the subject are available. See:

- Clemens Köttelwesch, ed., *Zur Katalogisierung mittelalterlicher und neuerer Handschriften*, Zeitschrift für Bibliothekswesen und Bibliographie, Sonderheft (Frankfurt: Klostermann, 1963).
- Otto Mazal, ed., *Handschriftenbeschriebung in Österreich: Referate, Beratungen und Ergebnisse der Arbeitstagungen in Kremsmünster (1973) und Zwettl (1974)*, Veröffentlichungen der Kommission für Schrift- und Buchwesen des Mittelalters, Rhe. 2, Bd. 1, Österreichische Akademie der Wissenschaften philosophisch-historische Klasse Denkschriften, 122 (Vienna: Österreichische Akademie der Wissenschaften, 1975).
- Maria Cecilia Cuturi, ed., *Il Manoscritto: Situazione catalografica e proposta di una organizzazione della documentazione e delle informazioni (Atti del Seminario di Roma, 11–12 giugno 1980)* (Rome: Istituto centrale per il catalogo unico delle biblioteche italiane e per le informaztioni bibliografiche, 1981).
- Ingo Reiffenstein, ed., *Beiträge zur Überlieferung und Beschreibung deutscher Texte des Mittelalters (Referate der 8. Arbeitstagung österreichischer Handschriften-Bearbeiter vom 25.–28. 11. 1981 in Rief bei Salzburg)*, Göppinger Arbeiten zur Germanistik, 402 (Göppingen: Kümmerle Verlag, 1983).
- Geneviève Grand, ed., *Les Manuscrits datés: Premier bilan et perspectives, Neuchâtel 1983 = Die datierten Hanschriften: erste Bilanz und Perspektiven, Neuenburg 1983*, Rubricae, 2 (Paris: CEMI, 1985).
- Helmar Härtel, et al., eds., *Probleme der Bearbeitung mittelalterlicher Handschriften*, Wolfenbütteler Forschungen, 30 (Wiesbaden: Harrassowitz, 1986).
- T. Gargiulo, ed., *Documentare il manoscritto: Problematica di un censimento (Atti del Seminario di Roma, 6–7 aprile 1987)* (Rome: Istituto centrale per il catalogo unico delle biblioteche italiane e per le informaztioni bibliografiche, 1987).
- *Catalogiseren van handschriften en oude drukken in België: Typologie, normen en automatisering. Lezingen gehouden op de vergaderingen van de Belgische Commissie voor Bibliografie, in de Koninklijke Bibliotheek Albert I, op 18 april en 12 decembre 1988 = Le Catalogage de manuscrits et d'imprimés anciens en Belique: Typologie, normes et automatisation. Communications présentés lors des réunions organisées par la Commission belge de bibliographie, à la Bibliothèque royale Albert Ier, les 18 avril et 12 décembre 1988*, a special issue of *Archives et bibliothèques de Belgique* 61 (1990).
- Menso Folkerts and Andreas Kühne, eds., *The Use of Computers in Cataloging Medieval and Renaissance Manuscripts: Papers from the International Workshop in Munich, 10–12 August 1989*, Algorismus, 4 (Munich: Institut für Geschichte der Naturewissenschaften, 1990).
- Hope Mayo, ed., *MARC Cataloguing for Medieval Manuscripts*, a special issue of *Rare Books & Manuscripts Librarianship* 6, no. 1 (1990).
- Wesley M. Stevens, ed., *Bibliographic Access to Medieval and Renaissance Manuscripts: A Survey of Computerized Data Bases and Information Services* (New York: Haworth Press, 1992).
- A. Džurova and P. Schreiner, eds., *Actes de la table ronde: principes et méthodes du catalouguage des manuscrits grecs de la collection du Centre Dujèev (Sofia, 21–23 août, 1990)*, Publications du programme de la cooperation entre le Centre "Ivan Dujèev," de l'Université "St. Kliment Ohridski" de Sofia, et l'Université Aristote de Thessalonique, 1 (Thessalonique: Aristoteleio Panepistémio Thessalonikés, 1992).
- *Metodologie informatiche per il censimento e la documentazione dei manoscritti (Atti dell'Incontro internazionale di Roma, 18–20 marzo 1991)*, (Rome: Istituto centrale per il catalogo unico delle biblioteche italiane e per le informazioni bibliografiche, 1993).

- Eva Nilsson Nylander, ed., *Clavis memoriae: Ett seminarium om datoriserad katalogisering av handskriftsmaterial (Svenska institut I Rom, 22–26 april, 1996)*, Kungl. Bilbioteket rapport, 23 (Stokholm: Kungl. Biblioteket, 1997).

Various national and institutional bodies have issued official codifications of rules for manuscript cataloging. Some of these rules are still in force, while others have been superceded or have simply passed into disuse.

- **France. Ministère de l'instruction publique, des beaux-arts et des cultes.**
  Léopold Delisle, *Note sur la rédaction des catalogues de manuscrits* (Paris: Plon, 1884); reprinted in *Bulletin des bibliothèques et des archives* 1 (1884): 94–109.
- **Österreichische Leo-Gesellschaft.**
  Regulativ für die Bearbeitung von Manuscripten-Katalogen (Vienna: Österreichische Leo-Gesellschaft, 1895).
- **Biblioteca Apostolica Vaticana.**
  "Leges quas curatores bibliothecae Vaticanae in codicibus Latinis recensendis sibi constituerunt," in Marco Vattasso et Pio Franchi de' Cavalieri, *Codices Vaticani Latini I: Codices 1-678* (Rome: Typis Vaticanis, 1902), x–xiv.
- **France. Ministère de l'education nationale.**
  Léopold Delisle, *Instructions pour la rédaction d'un catalogue de manuscrits et pour la rédaction d'un inventaire des incunables conservés dans les bibliothèques de France* (Paris: H. Champion, 1910).
- **Spain. Junta Facultativa de Archivos, Bibliotecas y Museos.**
  Instrucciones para la catalogaciòn de manuscritos, estampas, dibujos originales, fotografías y piezas de musica de las bibliotecas públicas (Madrid: Imp. de la "Revista de archivos," 1910).
- **Anglo-American Conference of Historians. Anglo-American Historical Committee.**
  "Report on Editing Historical Documents," *Bulletin of the Institute of Historical Research* 1 (1923): 6–25.
- **Biblioteca Apostolica Vaticana.**
  Norme per l'indice alfabetico dei manoscritti (Vatican City: Typis Vaticanis, 1938).
- **Bibliothèque nationale de France.**
  "Règles suivies pour la rédaction des notices du catalogue du fonds latin," in *Catalogue général des manuscrits latins*, 1 (Paris: Bibliothèque nationale, 1939), v–vii; supplementary rules regarding title, content, and codicology given in vol. 7 (Paris: Bibliothèque nationale, 1988), ix–x.
- **Commission per la Pubblicazione degli Indice e Cataloghi delle Biblioteche Italiane.**
  "Regole per la descrizione dei manoscritti," in Ugo Costa, *Codice delle biblioteche italiane* (Rome: Istituto poligrafico dello Stato, Libreria, 1949).
- **Spain. Dirección General de Archivos y Bibliotecas.**
  Instrucciones para la catalogación manuscritos, Anejos del Boletín de la Dirección general de archivos y bibliotecas, 34 (Madrid: Junta técnica de archivos, bibliotecas y museos, 1957.
- **Deutsche Staatsbibliothek. Zentrale Leiteinrichtung für Handschriften und Österreichische Akademie der Wissenschaften.**
  "Richtlinien und Terminologie für die Handschriftenbeschreibung," in *Handschriftenbeschreibung in Österreich: Referate, Beratungen und Ergebnisse der Arbeitstagungen in Kremsmünster (1973) und Zwettl (1974)*, ed. Otto Mazal, Österreichische Akademie der Wissenschaften philosophisch-historische Klasse Denkschriften, 122; Veröffentlichungen der Kommission für Schrift- und Buchwesen des Mittelalters, II,1 (Vienna: Österreichischen Akademie der Wissenschaften, 1975), 133–72.

- **Institut de recherche et d'histoire des textes.**
  Guide pour l'elaboration d'une notice de manuscrit, Bibliographies, colloques, travaux preparatoires: Serie informatique et documentation textuelle (Paris: C.N.R.S., 1977).

- **Inkunabeln. Kommission für Handschriften und Inkunabeln.**
  Ursula Winter, Renate Schipke, and Hans-Erich Teitge, *Regeln für die Katalogisierung von Handschriften* (Berlin: Deutsche Staatsbibliothek, 1983).

- **Centre international d'information sur les sources de l'histoire balkanique et méditerranéene.**
  Description et catalogage des manuscrits médiévaux, ed. O. Nikolèeva et al., Balcanica, 3, Études et documents, 3 (Sofia: Centre international d'information sur les sources de l'histoire balkanique et méditerranéene, 1984).

- **Society of American Archivists.**
  Stephen L. Hensen, *Archives, Personal Papers, and Manuscripts: A Cataloging Manual for Archival Repositories, Historical Societies, and Manuscript Libraries*, 2nd ed. (Chicago: Society of American Archivists, 1989).

- **Istituto Centrale per il Catalogo Unico delle Biblioteche Italiane e per le Informazioni Bibliografiche.**
  Guida a una descrizione uniforme dei manoscritti e al loro censimento, ed. Viviana Jemolo and Mirella Morelli (Rome: Istituto centrale per il catalogo unico delle biblioteche italiane e per le informazioni bibliografiche, 1990).

- **Deutsche Forschungsgemeinschaft. Unterausschuß für Handschriftenkatalogisierung.**
  Richtlinien Handschriftenkatalogisierung, 5th ed. (Bonn: Deutsche Forschungsgemeinschaft, 1992).

- **American Library Association / Library Association / Canadian Library Association.**
  Anglo-American Cataloguing Rules, 2nd ed., rev. (Chicago: American Library Association; London: Library Association; Ottawa: Canadian Library Association, 1998), chp. 4.

APPENDIX G: GLOSSARY

The following list consists only of those technical terms encountered in the text of *Descriptive Cataloging of Ancient, Medieval, Renaissance, and Early modern Manuscripts*. They are given only a functional definition here for use in conjunction with these guidelines and their definitions are not intended to be comprehensive or definitive beyond this context. More detailed information on these terms should be sought in appropriate specialized reference works, such as Denis Muzerelle, *Vocabulaire codicologique: répertoire méthodique des termes français relatifs aux manuscrits* (Paris: CEMI, 1985); Michelle P. Brown, *Understanding Illuminated Manuscripts: A Guide to Technical Terms* (Malibu, Calif.: J. Paul Getty Museum; London: British Library, 1994); or Marilena Maniaci, *Terminologia del libro manoscritto*, Addenda: Studi sulla conoscenza, la conservazione e il restauro del materiale librario, 3 (Rome: Istituto centrale per la patologia del libro, 1998). Other terms not specifically defined here are assumed to accord with those given in the glossary that accompanies *AACR2R*.

Autograph
A signature written by the individual to whom it belongs. Do not confuse with the subscribed attestation of an individual recorded by a scribe or notary, such as a witness in a legal document. See also HOLOGRAPH

Ascender
The upright stroke of a letter extending above the HEADLINE, *e.g.* as in **b**, **d**, and **h**.

Baseline
The line of writing (independent of the actual RULING) upon which the body or minim of a letter rests. In a block of text lacking frame-ruling, used as the extreme lower line from which the written space of a manuscript is measured. Elements of a letter extending below the baseline are called DESCENDERS. See also HEADLINE

Bifolium
A sheet of writing material (usually parchment, paper, or papyrus) folded in half to produce a pair of conjugate leaves. Multiple bifolia inserted into one another and sewn together through the fold make up a QUIRE.

Bulk date
Inclusive range of dates for the greatest concentration of items or works encompassed within a larger collection whose extreme dates exceed those of the greatest concentration.

Byname

The familiar name or nickname, as opposed to the official SHELFMARK, by which a famous manuscript is popularly known. Also known collectively as *ocelli nominum*.

Catchword

A word or phrase written in the lower margin of the verso of the last leaf of a QUIRE that corresponds to the first word or phrase of the following quire. Used as a device to ensure the proper ordering of quires when gathered together as a book. Orientation on the page is usually horizontal, but may also be vertical in later examples, or even diagonal. Catchwords may be plain or decorated. See also QUIRE SIGNATURE and LEAF SIGNATURE.

Chirograph

A document written in duplicate on the same sheet with the texts written in opposite orientation to one another and a space left between the texts where the word *Chirographum* (or some other word, phrase, or series of letters) was customarily, though not always, written, and through which a straight or indented cut was made separating the two halves and producing copies that were the physical counterparts of one another. Used as a means of authentication. Also commonly known as an indenture (when written in triplicate or quadruplicate known as an indenture tripartite or quadripartite).

Codex (pl. codices)

Form of the book composed of collected sheets of writing material (usually parchment, paper, or papyrus) folded double to form bifolia which are then gathered into quires sewn together through the center fold which are themselves then assembled into sequential order and usually provided with a protective cover. A codex may consist of a single quire or many, and contain one or many individual manuscripts.

Colophon

A statement, usually found at the end of a manuscript, though it may appear instead at the beginning, that provides information regarding the date, place, agency, or reason for production of the manuscript. Sometimes referred to as a subscription, particularly when only the scribe and date are specified. The colophon may be separate from or part of the closing rubric.

Composite codex manuscript

A manuscript codex composed of two or more physical parts of varying origin or date of production that have been subsequently bound together.

Descender

The upright stroke of a letter extending below the BASELINE, *e.g.* as in **p** and **q**.

Diplomatic transcription

A method of transcription used in the production of a diplomatic edition (distinct from a type facsimile) that attempts to represent by means of a system of editorial signs the physical state of an individual manifestation of the text of a work, reproducing original spellings, punctuation, and capitalization and showing all additions, suppressions, or substitutions made to the text at the time of and subsequent to its creation.

Dorse
The reverse or back of a letter or legal document.

Eschatocol
The concluding section of a legal document, such as a charter. In a public document, the eschatocol normally contains the attestation of the principal parties involved, witnesses, notaries, etc., and a dating clause indicating day, month, year, and place of execution.

Explicit
The closing words of the text proper of a work, exclusive of any closing RUBRIC that might follow it. Commonly the introductory word of the closing rubric, though *finit* is also used. Originally an abbreviation of the Latin *explicitus,* as in the phrase *explicitus est liber,* meaning "the book is unrolled," a usage taken over into the codex form of the book from the earlier roll. Used from the Middle Ages as a 3rd person singular verb meaning "here ends," the plural form being *expliciunt.*

Foliation
Sequential numbering of individual leaves. The front of the leaf is referred to as the recto (**r**) and the back as the verso (**v**).

Folio
As a term of codicological description, one of the paired leaves of a BIFOLIUM. As a term of bibliographical reference, may be applied to either one of the paired leaves of a bifolium or to a singleton. Abbreviated as fol. or fols.

Gathering
See QUIRE.

Gloss
Marginal or interlinear comment, citation, interpretation, translation, etc., the purpose of which is to explain or expand the meaning of a text.

Grade of script
The level of execution employed in the writing of a given type of SCRIPT, determined by the degree of care and rapidity (*ductus*) exercised in drawing its letter forms. Formal definition in the grades of script are applied most frequently within the Gothic system of scripts: *formata* (carefully and slowly drawn), *libraria* or *media* (drawn with medium care and speed), and *cursiva* (rapidly drawn).

Hand
The characteristics exhibited by an individual in the writing of a SCRIPT.

Headline
The line above which the bodies of letters within a line of writing rise no higher, i.e. excluding ASCENDERS.

Holograph
A manuscript in the handwriting of its author. See also AUTOGRAPH

Illumination
Any painted or penwork decoration (particularly gold or silver) used to adorn a manuscript, including such features as canon tables, calendars, carpet pages, author, donor, or evangelist portraits, miniatures, initials, borders, etc., but excluding such features as simple pen-flourished letters and line fillers, or the highlighting of letters or paragraph marks within a text usually executed in red or blue ink.

Incipit
The opening words of the text proper of a work, exclusive of any opening RUBRIC that might precede it, of sufficient length to identify the work uniquely. Frequently used during the Middle Ages as a means of reference to a work, or to a specific passage or chapter within a work, in place of a title. Also commonly the introductory word of the opening rubric. From the Latin *incipere*, meaning "here begins," the plural form being *incipiunt*.

Leaf
One of the individual units (FOLIO or singleton) making up a BIFOLIUM, QUIRE, or book. A leaf possesses a front and a back, described as recto and verso, and may contain writing or decoration on one or both sides, or neither. As a term of codicological description, it is referred to as a leaf, regardless of whether it is foliated or paginated. As a term of bibliographical reference, it is referred to as a folio if it has been foliated (with the recto or verso sides specified), or each of its sides is referred to individually as a page if it has been paginated.

Leaf signature
A combination of letters and numbers written on the recto of the first-half of the leaves of a QUIRE used as a device to ensure the proper ordering of quires within a book and leaves within a quire. The individual elements of the leaf signature designating the quire and the leaf are themselves sometimes referred to separately as the QUIRE SIGNATURE and the LEAF SIGNATURE.

Line Filler
A simple or decorated line or bar drawn to fill or justify any remaining unoccupied space in a line of text against a (usually) right margin.

Manuscript
From the Latin *manu scriptus*, meaning "written by hand." Both an adjective and a noun used to describe a method of production and its product: a book, letter, document, etc. written by hand, usually on parchment, paper, or papyrus. Use in distinction to CODEX to denote a component item making up part of a COMPOSITE MANUSCRIPT CODEX. As a noun, not applied to writing as inscribed on clay, stone,

etc., nor properly to items such as typescripts, mimeographs, or other mechanical or electronic means of substitution for handwriting.

Minim
The upright stroke of a letter standing between the BASELINE and HEADLINE, *e.g.* as in **m, n, u,** and **i.**

Opisthograph (alt. Opistograph)
A MANUSCRIPT containing writing on both the recto and the verso, but generally used only to describe a ROLL possessing this feature.

Pagination
Sequential numbering of each side, or page, of a LEAF.

Palimpsest
Any writing SUPPORT (parchment, paper, or papyrus) whose original text has been erased and which has been subsequently reused to receive other writing. The original text may still be visible or recoverable through the use of ultra-violet light.

Parchment
Generic term used to denote any writing SUPPORT material made from animal skin, such as sheep, goat, calf, etc. VELLUM is a term properly applied only to calf skin, which produces a very fine, white, and thin writing surface lacking the imperfections commonly found in the skins of other or older animals. However, owing to its qualitative associations the term vellum is frequently misapplied to writing support material from any animal that has been prepared to a similarly high level of quality. The term parchment is to be preferred in all cases.

Protocol
The opening section of a public legal document, such as a charter, normally containing the invocation, superscription, address, and salutation.

Quire
A gathering of usually two or more BIFOLIA (or combination of bifolia and singletons) inserted into one another and sewn together through the fold. One or more quires sewn together may comprise a CODEX.

Quire signature
A number or letter written on the verso of the last LEAF of a QUIRE that follows in sequence the number or letter of the preceding quire and is used as a device to ensure the proper ordering of quires within a book. Distinct from LEAF SIGNATURE. Also known as quire numeration.

Roll
Sheets of parchment, paper, or papyrus sewn or pasted to one another to form a continuous writing surface with the text oriented horizontally (usual in the case of papyrus) or vertically (usual in the case of parchment and paper) along the length of the roll.

Rubric

A heading, characteristically written in red ink, that either precedes a body of text and introduces the title of the work or its subdivisions (known as an opening rubric), or follows a body of text or its subdivisions and signals the conclusion of the work or subdivision (known as a closing rubric). An opening rubric normally begins with the word *incipit* and a closing rubric with the word *explicit*, though both are distinct from the INCIPIT and EXPLICIT as the opening and closing words of the text proper of a work.

Ruling

A combination of horizontal and vertical bounding lines drawn or incised in simple or complex patterns used to set out the written space on a page and to guide the line of writing across the page. Also describes the process of ruling. Ruling may be drawn in dry or hard point using a stylus (*i.e.,* "ruled in dry point"), in lead or silver point (*i.e.,* "ruled in lead," or " … in plummet," or "… in crayon," or "… in pencil"), or in ink using a pen (*i.e.,* "ruled in pen"). A text block enclosed in upper and lower horizontal and inner and outer vertical bounding lines is said to be frame-ruled.

Script

A system of lettering or writing that possesses discernable characteristic features and which is identifiable as a type. A model or standard that guides the drawing of letter forms by an individual scribe. See also GRADE OF SCRIPT and HAND.

Seal

An impression on malleable material, usually wax (sometimes metal, and later commonly shellac or a paper wafer), made by a matrix engraved with images or characters indicating personal or corporate identity and used as a means of authentication. Term applied equally to the impression as to the object itself as well. Attached to a document by cords or slips of parchment (pendant), or applied directly to a document (en placard).

Secundo folio

The first word or words of text appearing on the second leaf of a work or manuscript. Frequently cited in medieval (usually institutional) library catalogs as a means of distinguishing between multiple copies of the same work which share the same INCIPIT.

Shelfmark

A mark consisting of a combination of letters, numbers, or names usually indicating the physical location of a manuscript within a particular *fonds*, room, bookcase, or press and its position relative to other items on the same shelf or within the sequence of a collection. May also, or instead, possess topical signification or indicate accession or inventory order. In the past and today commonly used as the official designation for a manuscript and as the organizing principle for a manuscripts catalog.

Sign manual

A notary's device or mark used as a means of authentication.

Support
Material (usually parchment, paper, or papyrus) used to receive writing or decoration. Also known as material support or writing support.

Title page
Separate page at the beginning of a MANUSCRIPT given over predominantly to the display of the title and (usually) statement of responsibility of a work, or a text page at the beginning of a manuscript on which the title and statement of responsibility is physically distinguished from the text proper and appears more prominently than as simply part of the opening RUBRIC or as a running title.

Vellum
As a specific material designation (see 5C1), use PARCHMENT.

INDEX

Page numbers in italics refer to the examples in Appendix C and Appendix D.